BBC

LAURENCE LLEWELYN-BOWEN

CONTENDER
BOOKS

Based on the *Design Rules* programme produced by the BBC 2003

Series Producer, Mark Bristow
Director, Graham Strong

Design Rules and the Design Rules logo are trade marks of the British Broadcasting Corporation
and are used under licence. *Design Rules* © BBC 2002

By arrangement with the BBC

BBC and the BBC logo are trade marks of the British Broadcasting Corporation and are used under licence.
BBC logo © BBC 1996

First published 2003 by Contender Books
48 Margaret Street
London W1W 8SE
www.contendergroup.com/books

This edition published 2003
1 3 5 7 9 10 8 6 4 2

ISBN 1–84357–083–1

Researcher: Emma Clegg
Project Co-ordination: Julian Flanders (designsection), Rebecca Gee and Kate Gribble (Contender Books)
Designer: Carole McDonald
Picture Research: Alexandra Doel
Index: Indexing Specialists

Grateful thanks for interviews with, and notes taken from: Anabel Alton, Professor Janette Anderson and
Professor Oliver Braddick, Jill Blake, Dr Ione Fine, Professor Richard Gregory, Professor Barrie Gunter, iGuzzini labs,
Gina Lazenby, Vinny Lee, Professor Byron Mikeledes and Stephen Mullins.

Very many thanks also to all the BBC TV *Design Rules* crew, especially Mark Bristow, Graham Strong,
Claire Markwell, Wendy Bowden and Sylvia Mukasa, for all their help in the development of the book.

Design by designsection, Frome, Somerset
Colour separations by Radstock Reproductions Limited, Midsomer Norton, Somerset
Printed and bound in Great Britain by Butler & Tanner Limited, Frome and London

CONTENTS

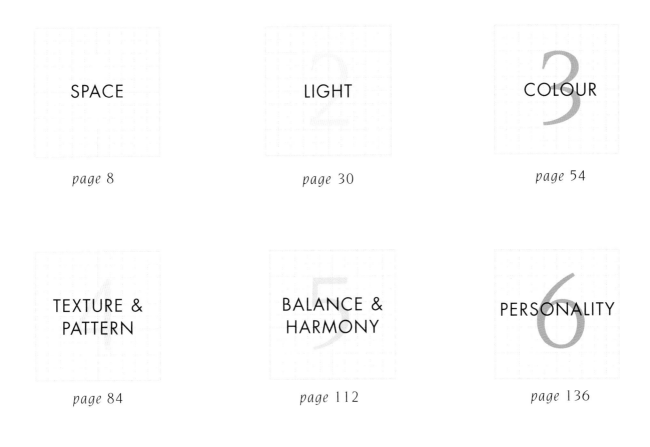

INTRODUCTION

The now-famous dictum by the modernist architect Le Corbusier (1887–1965) was that 'a house is a machine for living in'. What he meant by this was that architecture and living spaces should be streamlined, that every part of them should work towards achieving design perfection. His radical ideas were never implemented on a widespread scale, but we have learnt much from his methodology and vision. If we take his phrase literally and the house really is a machine for living in, then there should be rules to follow on every level. Rules, to pin down the artistic intricacies of interior design? Is this really possible?

All rooms are for living in, so they have a practical purpose. But they also stimulate us, make us feel a certain way, make us react to their features and designs. Indeed, we want them to do this, to create moods appropriate to the purpose of the space. This is where it

becomes complex, because how we react to what we see around us is a delicate interaction between science, psychology, and design vision. *Design Rules* will be looking at how we react to every aspect of our environment and will aim to draw general principles from its findings. These general principles will never be definitive. Design is an abstract business. It is also highly personal, and therefore subjective. But there are solid facts grounded in both design and science that can give you the ammunition to present your homes in the best possible light.

Historically, there has been a nervous relationship between art and science, but it is true that some of the most fascinating developments have come from the creative exploration of science and mathematics, art and metaphysics. The Renaissance painter Leonardo da Vinci (1452–1519) was also a sculptor, architect, engineer, mathematician,

scientist and philosopher and he developed revolutionary new theories on the use of perspective and colour that are still applied today. These different disciplines need not be seen in isolation. Sometimes their conclusions don't dovetail, but at other points they do. This book draws from scientifically proven facts, design theory and from alternative therapies and beliefs. They all help to build up a more complete picture of what we're dealing with, of how our homes actually work.

The reason that design rules are needed is that around 80 per cent of us live in small, badly lit spaces that were built between the middle of the nineteenth century and the present day. Many of them are designed to answer the social needs of a different historical era or to ensure a quick-profit building economy rather than to cater for modern living requirements. So when we look at houses in this book, we're not considering luxury homes and penthouse flats, for most of us only the stuff of dreams. Rather we're looking at what the majority of the British population have and that's compromising spaces – rooms with small or no windows, narrow passageways, awkward shapes, defunct features and, of course, a three-piece suite.

We are at an exciting point in design, a period when individual expression is emphasised above all else. Whether you yearn for a romantic floral hideaway, a white meditative space, an Oriental low-level living room or a corner to display your collection of plastic kitsch, then there are always basics to consider that will affect how well the space works. Those basics won't provide step-by-step guidance, because every space, and every person, is different. However, I hope we can guide you towards some of the answers to make your rooms fulfil every aspect of their potential.

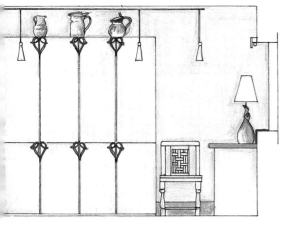

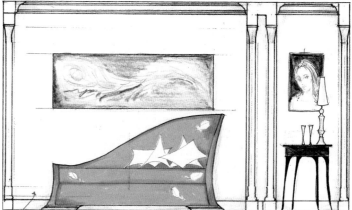

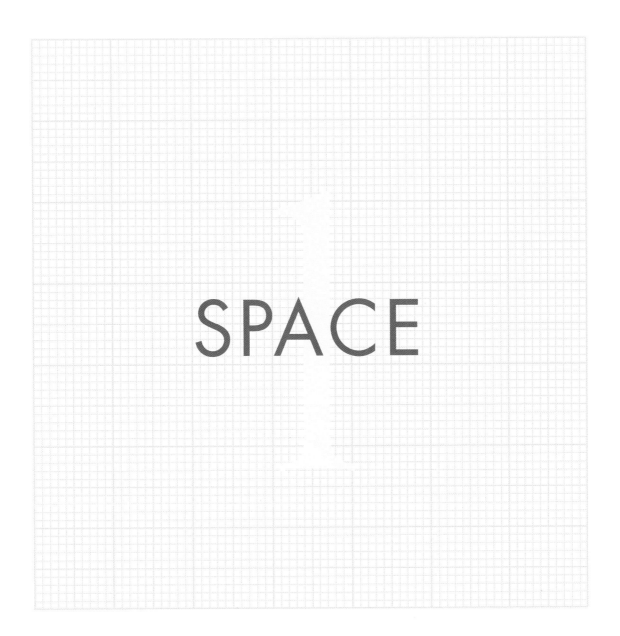

SPACE

design RULES

The majority of the British population live in formulaic spaces, with terraced houses such as these providing living spaces that are a mirror image of the neighbouring house. Built for the perceived standard requirements of the day, it can be a challenge to adapt such spaces to suit modern lifestyles.

Is it any wonder that space is at a premium? In the UK, population figures have increased from just over 40 million in 1901 to nearly 60 million 100 years later. And in 2002, the number of households in Britain overtook the number of available homes for the first time since records began. Whether your home is a converted one-bedroom ground-floor flat or a listed country cottage, a late twentieth-century modern home or a Victorian family terraced house, then there is no doubt that your space – and how you use it – matters. The main reason why people move house is to gain more space to accommodate their growing families and possessions: a larger kitchen, another bedroom, a second reception room. It is obvious that we all value extra living space, but what about understanding how to use what you have got to its very best advantage?

We're not looking here at the redefinition of space – knocking down walls or other structural changes – but working economically within the framework of your home and finding ways of showing it off to maximum effect. Without drastic and expensive building work there is no way of making your home bigger, but we have suggestions to guarantee that you can make it look and feel larger.

THE CHANGING ROLE OF LIVING SPACES

The history of domestic spaces has been constantly in flux, adapting with each century to respond to the styles and limitations of the day. Most medieval homes (1200–1450) were damp and dark places with small shuttered windows, often no chimneys and rarely more than one or two rooms with no defined spaces. In the Tudor and Elizabethan periods (until the beginning of the seventeenth century), homes were an important measure of social status, although privacy of any kind was exceptional. In the seventeenth century, overcrowding was still a problem for the ordinary population, with many families living in one-room houses that were shared with livestock and poultry. The rise of the merchant classes throughout the seventeenth and eighteenth centuries created an influential group who developed luxurious town houses. These homes provided formal, comfortable, well-equipped rooms with a defined purpose. A nobleman in the eighteenth century would even have used three bedrooms throughout the process of the night: a grand ceremonial space for bidding goodnight, a bedroom occupied by his wife or mistress, and a smaller chamber for his own private use.

The industrial revolution in the Victorian era meant that workers moved from agricultural activity based close to home, to work that involved commuting to factories: it was from this that our definition of home as a place of relaxation, nurture and socialising developed. Because so much of our housing stock is Victorian (25 per cent of our homes were built before 1919), the design influences of the era are ever present. Although ranging vastly in style and size – from grand town houses to small terraces of workers' cottages – they tend to be repetitive and orthodox in their structure and have formal self-contained rooms linked to specific activities.

Naturally, our homes also include those from the twentieth century, including 1930s' suburban council houses, the open-plan apartments of the 1950s, 1960s' and 1970s' high-rise apartments and the new-build housing of the late twentieth century. However respectful we are of the period of our home, it still needs to embrace our modern-day lives, which are more cellular than in the past: we eat meals at different times of the day, watch

television and listen to music in separate rooms to other family members. We no longer want small, single-function rooms, but family rooms that accommodate multi-purpose activities. There can therefore be a real tension between what we desire and the housing structures that we have inherited.

But, take courage, because whatever the format of your home, there are plenty of sprawling houses with poorly utilised and under-developed spaces and equally small flats that seem light and spacious simply because the spaces are well designed. It is all a question of creative presentation, heaps of loveliness and a few design rules.

The dining rooms of the past were often self-contained – rather than dining areas integrated with living rooms as we prefer them today. Here, in what was probably a farmworker's cottage, the dining area was part of the main living space with a kitchen area beyond. The back door was often used as the informal family entrance and exit, with use of the front door reserved for formal occasions.

ASSESSING THE POTENTIAL OF YOUR SPACE

Whatever the style and period of house you live in, your individual living areas will be divided by walls, ceilings and floors. These structural divisions are designed by an architect to create spaces that encompass the needs of those living there, providing at a basic level shelter and warmth, and at an emotional level home and security. The way that they are organised gives each room a particular quality: scale and proportion, light levels, textures and a relationship with the areas surrounding it.

In order to understand how to get the most from each of your rooms, then you need to evaluate the strengths and weaknesses that each space offers. To do this, simply walk in and, looking beyond the existing decoration and furnishing treatment, calmly assess what you see. Look at the dimensions of the room including the height, the size and position of the windows, where the light is coming from, and consider the use of the room. Note any elements that you need to work around, such as fireplaces, historical features and dominant furnishings that are essential to the room, such as a sofa, or a bed, or a desk and shelving area. Look at the room's focal points as they are now, and decide what isn't working well in the current use of space and why this might be. Architects are trained to design buildings in three dimensions and while you cannot match their experience and professional expertise, an awareness of these fundamental issues will give you the ammunition to creatively rethink how to use a space. Once you have done this, consider some of the ideas that follow.

SCALE

A 5 x 5m area is supposed to be one of the most useful room dimensions, being neither too big nor too small. You may be lucky enough to have one of similar dimensions, but it's equally likely to be long and narrow, L-shaped or a small square box. But scale is not just a question of width and length, think about the height of your room too, and whether the whole works proportionately or is far from ideal. If your conclusions are not inspiring, be reassured that there are many ways to change the perception of a space (*see pages* 18–23), by tricking the mind to increase or decrease the perceived proportions.

When it comes to furniture, many of us are guilty of preferring over-size furnishings such as engulfing, comfortable sofas, enormous wardrobes or large televisions – and then there's the stuff we inherit, which can also be huge. But do these pieces work in your room? Three-seater sofas, in fact, rarely have all three seats used. Faced with a sofa with two people sitting at each end, visitors would sooner stand about uncomfortably than sit down between them. It seems that this is because of our personal comfort zones, requiring approximately a one-metre distance between you and those to whom you are near. Psychologists say that this is because this is the distance at which we can see people's expressions clearly without having to move our eyes between eyes and mouth. If you are about to buy a large sofa for a small room, bear this in mind and consider scaling down your ideas, but if not, there are still ways of disguising elements that are too large. Placing a runner or folded throw down the middle of the sofa over the back and seat, for example, can break up bulky areas of sofa. An enormous television can be made into an effective focal point (*see Focal points on pages* 116–117) so that the room can support its dominance and there are many ways to integrate other bulky features with the way that you decorate your room (*see Visual contrast on pages* 76–77 *and Pattern and illusion on pages* 98–101).

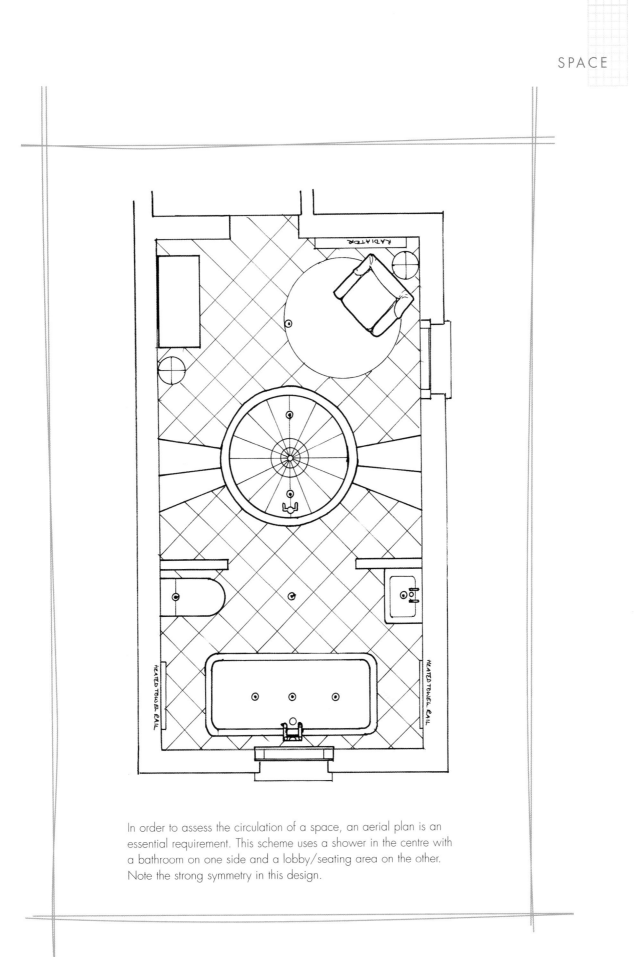

In order to assess the circulation of a space, an aerial plan is an
essential requirement. This scheme uses a shower in the centre with
a bathroom on one side and a lobby/seating area on the other.
Note the strong symmetry in this design.

DYNAMICS AND CIRCULATION

The circulation in a room should provide a comfortable passage around the furnishing elements in response to how the room is used. Think about creating an easy pathway between the door and the main activity areas of a room. If you have to step over a pile of books, veer round a chair, or squeeze yourself along your entrance hall between a bike and a chest of drawers, then the circulation isn't working. This may sound simple advice, but it's amazing how many people get it wrong. This is partly a matter of clearing up clutter (*see Avoiding clutter on page* 115) and finding solutions to storage problems, but it's also about planning. I always recommend doing a furniture plan, either to scale on paper or if practical in an empty room using newspaper cut to the exact shape of your furniture. Many people change the position of their furniture at intervals as a sort of furniture therapy, but there is almost always a single, most successful formation.

When planning circulation, you must take into account the main architectural features, or focal points. This is one of the most crucial dynamics of a space and yet their impact is often not consciously registered. If there are no focal points, then they should be introduced. The attention of someone entering the room should immediately be captured by an inviting interest point such as a lit fire. Such areas of interest tend always to revolve around light: windows, French doors, the fireplace and the television, the central feature in a great many living rooms. Avoid making the television the only main feature with seating clustered around it. Try to put it at one end of a room and introduce other interest and activity areas. Never block a door with seating or plants, and windows, even if they have a dismal view, should always have the most made of them. This is because humans love looking at light and are always drawn towards it.

For rooms used exclusively for dining, the circulation issues revolve around the relative proportion of the size of the table to the rest of the room and sensitively integrating other furnishing elements without detracting from the available seating space.

Windows also invariably offer views of the natural world, and if not that, at least a prospect beyond the limitations of the man-made environment. In the summer with its stronger light levels, people prefer to sit near the window, but in the winter with the greyer light and short days, a cosy spot near the fire will probably be the most appealing place to settle (*see also Focal points on pages* 116–117).

When designing a room, an interior designer aims for a balance between the practical uses of a room and the nature of the space. You should aim for no less. In the kitchen, circulation may already be defined by a built-in kitchen, which may or may not have the recommended essential triangle formation between fridge, cooker and sink within a three-step pace. But other mobile elements should still be designed around the way that you move through the room. If you have a long room or a larger space, you may need to think of your furniture arrangements within smaller groups along the length of the area. A study area in a bedroom needs to be more isolated from the sleeping area and next to natural daylight and a children's play area should be in an area where there will not be constant passing feet. How you enter a room may automatically divide it into different areas, so seating arrangements should be planned around this. Create three-dimensional patterns within the boundaries of your rooms, but always balance the practicalities with the aesthetic value of an arrangement.

The more available space around freestanding elements the better. This increases the feeling of space and allows easy access from one part of the room to another.

A cosy fire with seating clustered around it gives an immediate feeling of safety and enclosure. If you like intimacy such as this, a smaller size room can provide the perfect setting.

INDIVIDUAL SPACE REQUIREMENTS

All space is relative – to the purpose of the room and to the number of people who use it. Many private houses in the UK are designed for six or more people, but often just two or three people live there, involving a high circulation of space, which can be tiring and uneconomic. In the public sector, however, rooms are often too small for the larger families living there, leaving inadequate circulation, and personal space, for the inhabitants. The Austrian ethnologist Conrad Lorenz believed that social crowding leads to severe stress, demonstrated by the fact that too many rats in a cage will become frustrated and start fighting with each other. Having an adequate personal territory is actually an essential part of survival. Problems with lack of space are often created for us by living in houses

that were designed for a different era and a different way of living. So, we tend to prefer comfortable family rooms to relax in and to suit the needs of all who live there, not a formal front parlour for entertaining guests; and a family kitchen and dining area, not a small dark enclosed space at the back of the house for the exclusive preparation of food and a separate formal dining room for eating. We need, therefore, to find ways of adapting structures to suit modern lifestyles.

Space requirements are also relative to your size. If you have a small build, then a smaller room might suit your needs, making you feel protected and comforted. If you are larger and taller, however, then you may instead feel claustrophobic and trapped and won't have enough room to move around in. Larger spaces, too, can be difficult to manage and the loss of private areas and rooms for specific purposes, particularly in open-plan spaces, can also be unsettling and impractical. The fashion for loft conversions has given some people enormous spaces, broad and long and high, but they can be difficult to heat, appear stark and unsettling and create a feeling of vulnerability. It seems that this is because we don't like being approached from behind – given a choice in a restaurant, we opt to sit with our backs to the wall rather than facing away from the restaurant. This is also about intimacy: people prefer interaction with fewer people, otherwise our brain feels overloaded and unbalanced. This also depends on what we are used to – Californians, for example, live in big rooms and often find homes in the UK poky and restricting. UK citizens, however, tend to prefer the idea of enclosure, based on the nature of the houses that they live in and usually find enormous rooms unsettling.

If we don't live in houses designed in an open-plan style, we may have inherited rooms with knocked-through walls creating multi-purpose spaces. So, having assessed the space in our rooms and identified such problems, how do we overcome them? It all centres around creating a balance. What appeals to us most in any room is the idea of prospect and refuge: we need to be enclosed and soothed in our rooms, but also to look out beyond them towards daylight and, ideally, the natural world. This is why the idea of a fairy-tale turret room has so much appeal. So a room that is too small should be cleared until just the essential elements for the purpose of the room are there and the windows should be created as important focal points. The natural light should also be fully harnessed, using sheer blinds or curtains to shield any unattractive areas within its outlook. In larger spaces, we should sub-divide different activity zones, often within spaces previously defined by walls, so creating protected areas where we feel comfortable. This can be done by the placement and grouping of furniture and also by the reintroduction of gentle partitions, screens or curtains.

This open-plan modern space is probably converted from an old warehouse. The high ceilings allow the introduction of a mezzanine level and the large windows let the natural light flood in. Such roomy spaces with interconnecting activity areas, though, can make you feel vulnerable, allowing no feeling of safety and enclosure.

SPACE AND ILLUSION

If your space does not suit your lifestyle, then don't despair – the enormous advantage you have working in a space that seems to be unsuitable is that the mind is incredibly easy to deceive. We see the world in two-dimensions and our brains translate what they see into an awareness of the three-dimensional world. So you can fool your brain by manipulating the various cues that it uses to understand depth. The Ames Room at Techniquest in Cardiff, built to show how our eyes translate images to the brain, is a perfect example. This irregularly shaped room has the farthest wall tilted so that it lies at a significant angle to the floor and the decoration of the room is distorted to delude the brain into assuming that it is a square room. So, if two people of similar height stand at each of the far corners there are no depth cues and to the observer, one appears to be twice the height of the other. The same sort of brain adjustment happens in the empty room of an older house with sloping floors and ceilings. We assume that we are in a square room because that's what we expect, but will at the same time feel nauseous and unco-ordinated.

It has been found that we are conditioned to respond to vertical and horizontal lines because this is the nature of the man-made environments that we build and live in: babies as young as four months prefer looking at horizontal and vertical, rather than oblique, lines. Whereas with Zulu tribes who have no straight-line culture – living in round huts and even ploughing their land in curves – the effect is considerably reduced. It has also been found that those living in dense forests when taken to a built-up environment don't use receding lines as visual cues to depth because they have had a minimum of contact with square structures and therefore receding shapes. Based on their understanding of the world within their accustomed environment, they perceive forms in the distance as small, rather than far away.

One of the most useful tricks to delude the eye is based on this horizontal and vertical sensitivity. The simple rule is that vertical lines draw our eyes upwards and horizontal lines draw them across. So that in a room where you want to emphasise the height, use vertical lines in any form. This could be striped

The Ames Room at Techniquest in Cardiff shows how we rely on pattern cues to interpret space. The room is a wildly irregular shape, with the far wall at an angle to the floor and one of the far corners much further away than the other. Because of the distorted cues provided by the patterned elements and the lines of the windows and door, it appears that you are looking at a square room. When two people of equal size sit at each corner, therefore, one appears very much larger than the other.

Horizontal lines tend to be less frequently used on walls than vertical designs. They can, however, successfully elongate the length of the relevant wall and in the case shown here, camouflage the sharp angles of the corner.

wallpaper or other wallpaper with a straight vertical movement, painted vertical lines, column structures or forms, plaster mouldings, vertical niches, long curtains, even uplighters that form a column of light – such devices will all deceive the eye into thinking there is more height in the room than in reality. In a room that is narrow and long, horizontal lines have a similar effect, although this is a slightly less powerful prompt when compared to the vertical. You can use horizontal cues on the shorter wall and width of the room by laying floorboards across the room rather than along the length of it. This, combined with the use of advancing and receding colours, will dramatically broaden the room (*see also Colours that advance and recede on pages 60-63 and Pattern and illusion on pages 98–99*).

The power of the vertical and horizontal also connects to the idea of vanishing points and the acute angles on square structures that lead our eyes from the foreground to the far distance. If these lines are followed to their convergence point, this marks the point of the horizon, or eye level. This is a particularly sensitive level at which to use horizontal cues, perhaps with a series of pictures along a wall aligned at eye level. Such decorative devices stretch and squeeze our perception of a given space and give a room a more balanced proportion and therefore make those living in it feel more at ease.

The proportional placement of dado and picture rails also plays with our perception of space. Installing a dado lower than normal will make the ceiling seem higher. Similarly, using a wider skirting board or using a skirting with the same finish as the floors will make the ceiling seem lower.

To accommodate this need for straight lines and right angles, it can be a good idea in an awkwardly shaped room such as an attic to install a false, dado-height wall to give a vertical surface and flatten off irregular corners at floor level. You may lose a few feet of floor area, but it will feel bigger.

Windows will always lead the observer's eye away from a room. This is largely because of the power of natural light, but also because the idea of a prospect beyond the confines of a room is tremendously attractive. The windows here, reaching right up from floor level, extend the space by bringing the garden outside into the interior.

There are other ways of changing the way space is seen based around the way we understand perspective. In the Renaissance, artists such as Brunelleschi, Leonardo da Vinci, Piero della Francesca and Masaccio for the first time used the mathematics of one- and two-point perspective to give a strong illusion of three-dimensional form, and therefore depth, to their paintings. Their work was based around the idea of using the canvas as a grid following mathematical rules, with oblique lines showing the receding movement from the close front part of a structure to the back in the distance. We can play with this illusion by using decoration with grid forms or with the use of other aligned square features, such as tiles. The key is that the smaller the squares that you are creating, then the larger the space appears. This tiling trick is often used in bathrooms, but learn to understand it as a device to emphasise or de-emphasise (because all these tricks can be used in reverse) the spacial elements of a room.

BORROWING SPACE

Another trick is to trade on our love of windows and natural light, almost without exception the most instantly attractive feature as we enter a room. As long as we feel protected, we love to look out beyond our immediate environment and to sit near windows (which is why window seats in cafés are all taken first or office desks next to windows are the most popular). Natural light plays a significant role in the definition of space (*see Maximising and controlling natural daylight on page 38–39*), but another suggestion is to use space from outside a room, what the Japanese call 'borrowing landscape'. We can do this by removing any bushes or trees or other physical obstructions immediately next to a window that block our vision, and lead the eye outwards by creating a natural source of interest. Again, this frees the brain from the tight dimensions of the room and breaks the lines that define it.

This can also be done in the interior by running one room into another. Use the same flooring in an adjoining passageway or room to lead the eye through to a new area, create new points of interest and prevent the observer from feeling enclosed. You could also run a light wooden floor from one room through to the next and continue it up to skirting board level (*see On location on pages 24–28*), or paint skirting boards in the same colour as the floor or floor covering. This creates continuity, leads the eye to think of both rooms as one, as well as blurring the edges of each room and making the observer think that the floor is a larger surface – to the overall benefit of the space.

The technique of using the same flooring for adjacent rooms extends the perception of each individual room's size. This is because the eye continues to move freely through beyond the doorway. In this case, with the doors opened so wide, the adjoining room becomes an integral part of the space.

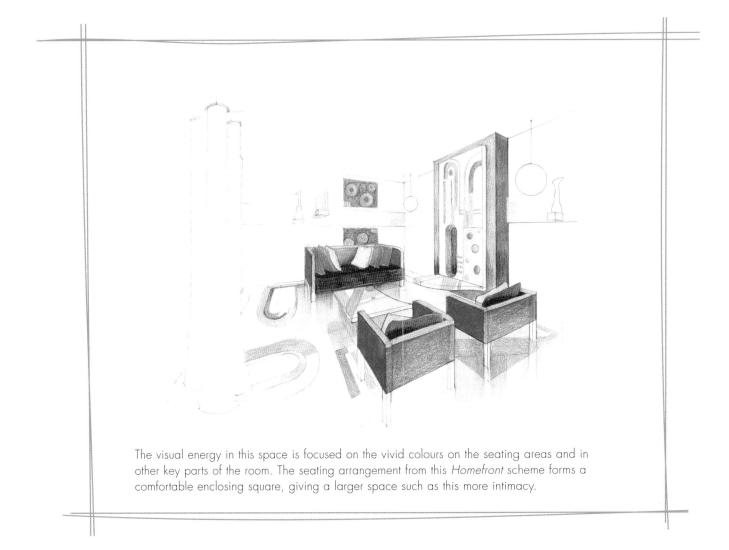

The visual energy in this space is focused on the vivid colours on the seating areas and in other key parts of the room. The seating arrangement from this *Homefront* scheme forms a comfortable enclosing square, giving a larger space such as this more intimacy.

REBALANCING ELEMENTS TO EXTEND SPACE

If you have a room that is too small, then always try to blur the edges and corners. This is because if the eye sees the lines representing the edge of the floor then it can define the exact parameters of the space and establish that it is tiny. Do this by breaking up the lines created by floor and walls with pieces of furniture that distract the eye from the edge of the room. Keep your furniture at right angles (rather than slanting angles) to the walls; avoid having all your furniture lined against the walls and draw furniture elements such as tables or sofas a little away from the walls into the room. Not necessarily so you can walk behind them – just so you can see space beyond them. Although you might think this will limit the space in the middle of the room, it is only a matter of a few centimetres and the more light and air that you have around your furnishings, then the greater the perception of space will be.

In the same way, sofas and comfortable chairs that don't have visible legs and are set almost flush to the floor appear as much more bulky and demanding of space than those with legs where you can see the floor beneath them.

This doesn't mean you should immediately rush out and buy a new sofa with legs, because these are all individual subtle cues that our eyes and brains react to. However, taken as a whole they have a dramatic impact on perception. Most crucially with a small room, you need to attract attention to the middle of the space, shifting the emphasis away from how small a room is by diverting the eye with dramatic focal points that are away from the edges, such as a rug in a contrasting colour to the floor. Drawn to the centre in this way, the mind, being occupied, assumes that the edges of the space are more distant (*see also Focal points on pages* 116-117).

Another way of rebalancing elements to make your space work better is to rehang certain doors so that they open in a direction that is most flattering to the room. It is surprising how many doors open to close down the main view into a room and other points of interest or don't open properly because of furniture placed just behind them. Rehanging the door will involve changing the direction of the lock and hinges and creating new notches for the hinges. You may also need to change the position of the light switch to the other side of the door – but believe me, it's well worth the effort.

The perception of space will be increased by drawing a table away from the edge of the room and having chairs all around it. This also makes it a friendlier social area, allowing the potential to sit in an enclosing square.

ON LOCATION

The small dimensions (3.7 x 4m) of the west-facing living room in this 1980s' Barratt-style home make the decoration and the organisation of space a real challenge. The walls had a decorative dado border with apricot painted above and terracotta below, the white ceiling had a textured Artex surface and the room was carpeted in a dark green. There were two navy-blue leather sofas with dark cushions and the curtains were dark green with floral motifs. The overall impression was dark and featureless and the dimensions, including a low ceiling, gave the room a claustrophobic feel.

The most essential requirement was to introduce colours that would increase the feeling of space and light. The ceiling was replastered to achieve a smooth finish (texture on any surface will always distract the eye and in this case was also creating shadows that made the ceiling appear lower). The ceiling was then painted white and the walls a pale blue. Apart from white, which may have been too stark in this space, pale blue, imitating the colour of the sky that we associate with the far distance, is the next most effective colour for making surfaces recede. The pale blue colour was taken right up to the top of the coving and the ceiling was painted white to give the room extra height. The main wall between the entranceway and the doors through to the kitchen had a painted block of slightly paler blue, framed by the pale blue used elsewhere: this gives a subtle visual impression of a window, as if the viewer is looking through to another plane. A picture light was also added to the centre of this wall.

A white storage unit was built running the length of the wall under the window to house the television and music system along with other electrical accessories which had been cluttering up the window side of the room. The white colour of this unit also serves to reflect dramatically more light into the room. A pale fabric blind that can be drawn up fully was used in the window to maximise daylight.

Pale wood laminate flooring was laid the length of the room running right through to the adjacent kitchen, a device that effectively blurs the parameters of the room and 'borrows space' from the kitchen. The same laminate boards also ran along the skirting to disguise the exact point at which the floor finishes and deceive the eye into thinking the room is larger.

The two sofas used by the occupiers restricted the space too much, so one was removed. A throw was used on the remaining sofa to break up the bulky shape and the dark colour. Several centres of interest were created in various parts of the room to distract and stimulate the attention of the observer, including well-placed framed pictures, one under the picture light. Two mirrors were also sited opposite the window, an unfailingly successful visual trick to reflect light back and make the space seem significantly larger.

The foliage outside the window blocked the view from the window and so was pruned back to give a more extensive prospect. (In a similar situation, you might also consider moving shrubs such as this to give a much more open view.) A sculptural green plant was potted in a blue pot and sited just beyond the window, with two indigo blue bottles just inside the pane to guide the eye outwards.

DESIGN RULES

The eye is drawn to focal points. Assess the main structural focal points in each room, such as windows and fireplaces, introducing new ones if appropriate.

Perception of space is based on body size. Different size spaces suit different size people: one person's claustrophobic box is another's cosy nest.

Aim to create both a prospect and a refuge in each room so you can feel enclosed, but also have a view beyond to the outside or natural world.

Plan your furniture with a scale drawing of your room or cut shapes to size and place them in the room to work out the best possible arrangement of elements.

Ensure that the circulation passageway through a room follows an easy and economic pathway from the door to all the other main activity areas.

Clutter closes down space, so edit your clutter to avoid blocking both circulation and reducing the perceived size of a room.

In large or long spaces, subdivide different activity zones to give definition to each part of the room.

When planning decoration and lighting, work with the principles that vertical lines draw our eyes up and horizontal lines draw them across to extend or reduce the proportions of a room.

Wallpaper with a square grid or tiling a room in squares will give the impression that it is bigger than it is – the smaller the grid, the larger the room appears.

Borrow space from outside by ensuring an unencumbered view of the outside world, and also from adjoining rooms by using the same flooring surface.

When furnishing small rooms blur the edges of the room to break up the lines between floor and walls; draw furniture a little way away from the walls; buy furniture in proportion to the room; choose furniture with legs.

Disguise oversize sofas by breaking up their upholstered surface with a different coloured or textured runner or folded throw.

LIGHT

any cultures think of light as representing life itself. The Spanish expression *dar a luz*, meaning 'to give birth' is literally translated as 'to give light'. Expressions such as 'I see the light', 'feeling in the dark' and 'being in a black mood' clearly show how essential light is to our understanding of the world and to our survival. Light is also the principal element that animates interior space and one of the most fundamental issues to consider when planning the design of an interior. There are two aspects to using light: the first is harnessing the available natural light to best effect (*see page* 38) and the second is using artificial lights to compensate for deficiencies in the former, to change the perception of a space or to create a particular mood (*see pages* 40–47). Any lighting decisions you make should be based on an overall scheme, because each different element contributes to a whole impression rather than just doing a localised job. We're also looking here at the basic science of light and how it affects us, because understanding how we react to light has a direct bearing on how we should use light in our homes.

Natural daylight floods into this generously proportioned space. Light has tremendous power over our mood, and therefore over the atmosphere of our interior spaces.

Most of our housing stock has a limited lighting allocation. In rooms with single windows, other areas of the room will be plunged into shadow. In the past, kitchens were typically dark, often windowless, as they were seen as servant areas and therefore as less important.

HOW WE REACT TO LIGHT

The way that we react to light is inseparable from how we see colour, as colours are perceived according to the light conditions surrounding them. White light, or ordinary daylight, is made up of all the spectral colours – red, orange, yellow, green, blue, indigo and violet – and each one represents light of a different frequency, red being the longest wavelength and violet the shortest. When white light falls on an object, the surface absorbs certain wavelengths of light and reflects others and the colour of the reflected light is what we see as the object colour. Which wavelengths are absorbed and which are reflected depends on the surface pigmentation of the viewed object. So, a tomato is red because it absorbs the blue and green light and reflects back the red light; grass is green because it absorbs the red and the blue light and reflects back the green; and a banana is yellow because it absorbs the blue light and reflects the red and the green (the combined activity of the two giving yellow). While this process is going on, a different part of the eye simultaneously detects the intensity

of light. The colours that we see are caused both by the colour of the light source and by the ways the objects that we see redirect light from elsewhere. This shows us that if we control light conditions, the way that we use both natural and artificial lighting can significantly change how we perceive objects within an interior.

Not all types of white light are spectrally well balanced: daylight changes constantly throughout each day and year (*see pages* 36–37) and methods of artificial lighting vary considerably. The human visual system has no problems combating this in order to recognise objects. It can instantly adapt to all sorts of light conditions and can detect fractional differences in light and see an object as the same colour both on a bright day and in a badly lit room. The impact of different light sources in our homes should not be underestimated, however. Incandescent tungsten bulbs (standard light bulbs), for example, cast a warm glow whereas fluorescent bulbs are characterised more by their cool light and each can be used to create a different atmosphere (*see Different qualities of artificial light on page* 40).

WHY WE NEED LIGHT

Because we are reliant on light to see, gloomy rooms make it hard for us to interpret our environment and make us feel uncomfortable. Many adults as well as children are frightened of the dark and it's quite possible that this aversion may have primeval roots – if there is no light then you can't detect any advancing threat, such as a poisonous snake or spider. Throughout history and before the invention of effective artificial lighting, humans were closely attuned to patterns of sunlight throughout the year, so they were active and worked during daylight hours and rested and slept after dusk.

Attitudes to daylight in the home have varied enormously throughout history. At one extreme, the enlightened ancient Greek and Egyptian civilisations planned the direction of their homes to use the warmth of the sun in winter and to protect them from the direct light of summer, with high windows to let heat escape during the day and cool air enter at night. The Victorians in the nineteenth century, however, positively disapproved of daylight, intent on shielding their fabrics and furnishings from fading and protecting their pale complexions, a skin colour that separated the ruling classes from the working populace. Victorian kitchens and bathrooms often had tiny windows or none at all, these rooms were considered less important because they were used by servants rather than the main family, a fact that may register with people living in Victorian homes. It was not until the 1920s that Coco Chanel famously made suntan glamorous and after this daylight was considered as fashionable and associated with health-giving benefits.

As well as being received through our eyes, light is also absorbed through our skin. The amount and the quality of light that we receive controls the pigmentation of the skin as well as the body's levels of vitamin D and calcium. The light around us also affects our glands: the pineal gland which produces melatonin, the sleep hormone; the hypothalumus which controls our emotions; and the pituitary gland, linked to a number of other hormones such as those controlling growth and thyroid function. If we don't get enough light, then these glands don't function effectively and we can suffer from a condition called Seasonal Affective Disorder (SAD), or winter lethargy. The symptoms of SAD include tiredness, withdrawal, depression, overeating, lack of concentration and sleeplessness. Studies have shown that the number of people affected increases according to their distance from the equator: 11 per cent of the British and Swedish population are affected by the condition as opposed to just one per cent in Saudi Arabia and Argentina. SAD typically runs from September until April when it lifts as the daylight hours increase and the quality of light becomes stronger, and its symptoms are heightened during November, December and January when the days are shorter. Our modern lifestyles dictate that we spend between 75–90 per cent of our time indoors, so it is hardly surprising that we are affected by this condition.

Our understanding of the physiological effects of SAD, the emphasis by alternative concepts such as Feng Shui on having maximum contact with daylight to nourish and protect us, alongside the fashionable use of glass in modern architecture mean that many people now aspire to live in a world that is dominated by glass and natural daylight.

Opposite: Such modern light-filled spaces are unlikely to be linked with those susceptible to a condition called SAD or Seasonal Affective Disorder, meaning that sufferers are not getting enough natural light. The problem is much more acute in areas of the world with fewer hours of sunshine.

ASSESSING YOUR QUALITY OF LIGHT AND HOW IT CHANGES

Daylight hours depend on where you are in relation to the equator and what time of year it is. In the UK, the sun rises in the east, moves overhead at a maximum angle of 62 degrees in the summer and sets due west. The south of England has about 16 hours of daylight in June and July, but only eight hours in December and January. Lerwick, in Shetland, has about four hours more daylight at midsummer than London and on the longest day it gets no lighter than twilight in the north of Scotland. The quality of light in Scotland is also much softer than the south of England. As well as having longer hours, the quality of light is of a much greater intensity throughout the UK during the summer months.

Because of our temperate but generally overcast climate, light here is often grey, usually tinted with green once it has reflected off fields, trees and grass.

So how does all this have a bearing on your home? Well, in order to plan your interior, in particular your lighting and colour schemes, no matter how delightful the proportions of your room, you need to understand what sort of daylight your home gets and how it changes throughout the day. This will depend in what direction your windows face. Windows facing east will offer a warm, bright light with morning sunshine creating long shadows and will lose direct light from the sun later in the day. South-facing windows have the best light qualities: a warm light that constantly changes

TRACKING THE SUN

EAST-FACING WINDOW

Stronger, low morning sunlight creating long shadows

Losing direct heat as sun moves away

SOUTH-FACING WINDOW

At midday in summer, sun reaches max angle of 62°

Warm light that changes throughout the day – sun is lower in the winter throughout the day, in winter reaching deep into the living space and in summer brighter but with a shallower reach. The brightness of the midday light from the south, closest to pure white light, can be strident and flatten out elements in a room. West-facing windows get sunlight at the end of the hottest part of the day in the early afternoon and this light can create glare. The late afternoon sunlight from the west then shifts to a softer illumination and the long shadows increase the feeling of depth. A northern window will get very little direct sunlight, offering a clear, consistent light with no brilliant glare, but it will have a cold edge. This light is preferred by artists as it is most reliable and creates no distracting shadows. Northern light can, though, create reflective glare if sited opposite a light-coloured building or one with lots of glass.

Many houses are not built directly facing these main points of the compass, so observe how the light changes throughout the day in your rooms, and remember that sky conditions vary constantly, affecting the quality of daylight that reaches your home. There are two general principles: firstly, north- and east-facing windows make it important to maximise the quality and quantity of daylight in a room and may require artificial lighting to enhance light and require measures to control glare. Secondly, south- or west-facing windows will receive a much better quality and quantity of daylight, but can still benefit from devices to control the amount of light entering the room.

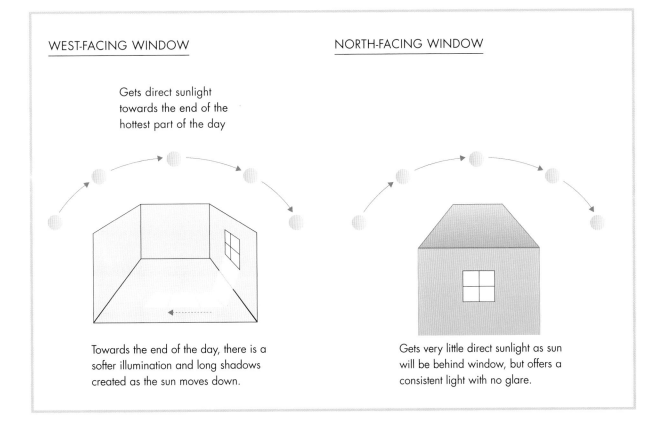

WEST-FACING WINDOW

Gets direct sunlight towards the end of the hottest part of the day

Towards the end of the day, there is a softer illumination and long shadows created as the sun moves down.

NORTH-FACING WINDOW

Gets very little direct sunlight as sun will be behind window, but offers a consistent light with no glare.

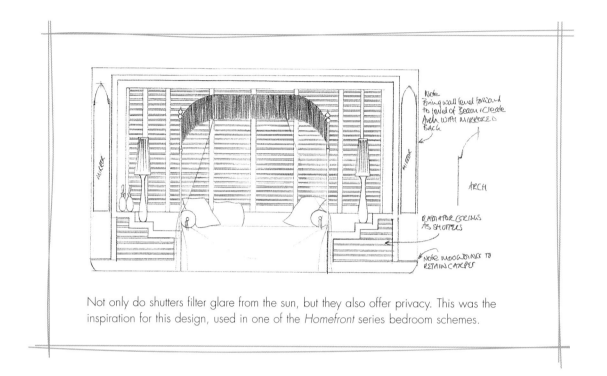

Note
Bring wall level forward
to level of Beam + create
Arch with mirrored
back

ARCH

RADIATOR GRILLS
AS SHUTTERS

Note moogoinge to
retain carpet

Not only do shutters filter glare from the sun, but they also offer privacy. This was the inspiration for this design, used in one of the *Homefront* series bedroom schemes.

MAXIMISING AND CONTROLLING NATURAL DAYLIGHT

We have seen that we need to maximise our contact with natural daylight. As well as trying to spend more time outdoors, there are a number of ways to harness daylight more effectively in our homes. The most basic approach is to avoid unnecessarily blocking windows, glass doors and the panes surrounding them. So, clean your windows regularly inside and out, avoid heavy curtains that block light, draw curtains back fully during daylight hours and avoid high or substantial furniture in front of windows and external glass doors in any area that blocks the natural daylight reach. Try to organise your space so it allows window seating or activity areas close to the window (such as a home office area) but without blocking the daylight in other parts of the room. If you are prepared to make slight structural adjustments, you can also raise the height of windows (far more effective for maximising daylight than widening them), use doors with translucent glass and introduce glass panes in doors that don't have them. Don't forget that the outside area beyond external glass doors and windows can also be adjusted, so trim or move any trees and plants that overshadow your windows and use deciduous trees and shrubs to increase the amount of winter sunlight.

The other way of increasing light is to use reflective surfaces. You can dramatically enhance

Any reflective surfaces, such as these areas of stainless steel, will bounce the available natural light around the room and increase the overall light level.

both natural and artificial light by avoiding dark, matt colours; using light decorations, furniture and floor-coverings; choosing light, reflective paint colours; and including mirrors and mirrored furniture to bounce light around a room. (A light meter test in the same room illustrates the effect of reflective and non-reflective surfaces: when the floor was painted white a light meter detected over double the amount of light available with a pale laminate flooring, and over four times more light than was available with a deep red carpet.) Outside devices to increase the reflection of light are to lay light paving underneath windows or to paint walls and fences opposite windows a light colour to reflect more light indoors. Finally, you can use full-spectrum bulbs, designed to mimic the colour spectrum of natural daylight, to counter any severe deficiency in natural light.

But maximising daylight is not the only challenge: all windows can be affected by glare (whether direct or reflected) so you may need to control the natural levels of sunlight in order to keep conditions comfortable in a room. Glare is a result of extreme contrasts in light intensity causing over-stimulation of the eyes and can lead to fatigue and loss of concentration. One of the most practical solutions for minimising daylight glare is to use blinds and shutters. These are available in many different materials and have either vertical or horizontal louvers that can deflect daylight and can be adjusted to changing light conditions. Light-diffusing curtains and blinds will also reduce glare and help protect fabric and furniture from fading.

Another idea is to use tinted glass or window films to give built-in shading qualities to lessen the quantity of daylight passing through it and reduce the amount of heat from the sun. Window films also have ultraviolet light absorbers, blocking harmful ultraviolet rays. Glare can also be reduced by planting shrubs outside or using potted plants inside to impede direct sunlight.

Blinds should be chosen specifically to deal with particular light conditions. The blind above provides a diffused lighting, giving a soft glow to the interior and successfully shielding any unsightly views beyond. Solid window shutters such as those shown below can be effective to block glare, but offer more inflexible levels of light filtering.

DIFFERENT QUALITIES OF ARTIFICIAL LIGHT

An object's true colour is best revealed in full-spectrum white light, but artificial light is rarely pure. In any case, pure white light can be severe, reduce contrast and give a bland, unflattering, regular light distribution that steals excitement and texture from a space. The spectrum of most lights tends either to have a red and yellow, or a blue and green character. This is because their light only uses a narrow band of the visual spectrum. This spectral emphasis can therefore be used to create particular moods: with red- and yellow-tinted light creating an associated mood of cosiness and warmth and blue and green tinted light creating a mood of serenity and coolness. Fast-food chains often use warm incandescent lights to entice their customers in, but have cooler blue lights in the dining area so they are not encouraged to stay too long. The idea of using light to create particular moods should also be considered for more functional areas, such as kitchens and bathrooms. You want to be able to see what you are doing in a kitchen, but not necessarily with lighting that creates a harsh, unsubtle glare in the room.

The intensity of light is another important factor in creating a successful space, both to suit particular activities and to present all parts of room in their most flattering aspect. The advantage is that whereas natural light will fluctuate constantly throughout each year and each day, artificial lights have a dependable constant light that can be adjusted to suit the purposes of a room.

Most fast-food chains use warm incandescent lights in the main serving area to attract their customers in and cooler lighting levels in the dining area to encourage them to move on quickly.

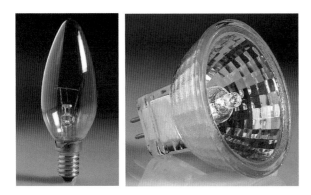

LIGHT BULBS

There are two aspects to artificial lighting: the actual source of the light (the bulb or lamp) and the light fitting by which it is presented. The bulb controls the light level, the light quality and the direction of light, whereas the fitting or shade will affect how it interacts with the room.

Standard filament light bulbs made from tungsten, or incandescent light sources, emit a yellow/white light from their centre in all directions, with a brighter, stronger light if the bulb is clear glass and a softer diffused light if it is opaque. These kinds of bulbs tend to show colours more accurately and they have an appealing warm quality. Tungsten lights are good when it is dark, but less effective during the day. They are cheap but have a low efficiency and come in many shapes and sizes, from golf-ball to candle shapes and with various fittings, from bayonet to screw. Halogen lights are filament bulbs containing halogen gas and are cooler than tungsten, but produce a bright, warm light reminiscent of sunlight. For this reason, they can be good in a north-facing room and for use when reading or using a computer. They generate a considerable amount of heat, so have to be used with fittings that can support these temperatures, although they use half as much energy for the same quality of light as a standard filament bulb. They are available either in low-voltage or mains-voltage form: the lower voltage ones are combined with a transformer and allow the design flexibility to create slimmer and smaller products; the mains-voltage ones give tremendous power and light colour without a transformer. Halogen lights are more expensive than tungsten, but have a considerably longer life. There is also a tungsten-halogen light with the same bright, white light. Another bulb, called Xelogen, a combination of xenon and halogen, is now available and growing in popularity because of its crisp, accurate lighting quality. This has an equivalent light output to halogen, but the light has a more yellow quality.

Fluorescent lights have gases contained in a tube, rather than a filament. Although they tend to be associated with the strip lights used in public institutions and warehouses, their size and efficiency has been revolutionised (they no longer visibly flicker or hum) and a wide range of designs are available. They spread light effectively over a large area and work well where a flat-wash light is needed. Compact fluorescent lights (CFLs) have a smaller, and more flexible, light source. Fluorescent light is often cold, but the colour can be improved with the use of warm white lamps. The colder types are useful in a loft or workshop setting, or choose a warmer yellow for a softer effect in your main living area. Diffuser shades are also available to soften glare.

There are also daylight bulbs, which are incredibly energy efficient, but vary tremendously in their effectiveness: these aim to closely emulate natural sunlight using the full colour spectrum. There are coloured lights and fibre optic lights from which to choose, too, but these should be used in a room as decorative dramatic statements rather than a crucial aspect of a scheme.

Unsurprisingly, certain types of light are used in different climates: for example, warm tungsten lamps are a definite favourite in the UK and cooler blue lights are more popular in the Middle East.

Lighting features within interconnecting areas such as passageways and stairwells are often forgotten. These low-voltage lights raise the light level on the stairway and act as dramatic accents.

LIGHT FITTINGS

These can produce an even distribution of light, project light in a particular direction with diffused light around or focus all the light in a constant directional beam. Before deciding on which suits you, establish the purpose of the light and how the quality of the light you are considering will link with the rest of the scheme (*see also Layers of artificial light on pages* 44–45). When selecting shades remember that a transparent shade will increase the light distribution, a translucent shade will give light with a gentler glow and an opaque shade will

channel the light towards its widest opening. A fabric shade in pleated form will create a more subtle statement and a more diffused light than one with regular edges. You might even choose one with a cut-out decoration that will reflect patterned light.

Don't forget the scale of your light fittings. A lampshade should be in proportion to its base in the same way as the lamp should be in proportion to the interior. Generally, the height of a shade should be similar to the distance from the base of the light to the bulb socket. The shade should also be at the very least as wide as the widest part of the light stand and the bottom of the shade should cover the socket. Also, think about their height and adaptability in relation to how you are using them – a bedside reading light, for example, must be high enough to illuminate the pages of the book. When lamp bases have reflective qualities, then they will reflect and maximise the light, so select these materials according to how much light you would like reflected.

LIGHT SWITCHES AND DIMMERS

Switches should always be positioned in the most convenient spot, next to the door or next to the activity that you need the light for. To achieve maximum efficiency, they should be planned around the way that you move through a room and through a house, with each switch at strategic points to control lights that you need to find your way further forward. For flexibility of mood, dimmers are an essential choice. These can be used in incandescent lights and most tungsten and halogen lights, but only particular types of fluorescent light. When installing a dimmer, you'll need to check that it has the power to carry the load on the circuit. I would recommend having dimmers on table lights as well as for more general lighting and this will require a twin circuit.

This subdued lighting scheme creates a relaxed mood in this sleeping area. The accent lighting around the bedhead balances effectively with the stronger white light filtering through the paper screens beyond.

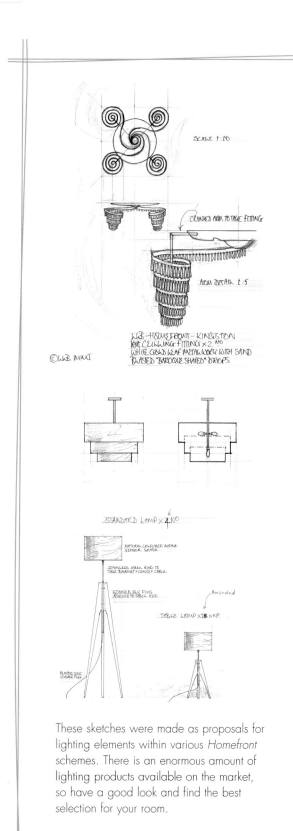

SCALE 1:10

CRANKED ARM TO TAKE FITTING

ARM DETAIL 1:5

© WRB MMII

WB HOUSE FRONT - KINGSTON
ROOM CEILING FITTING x 2 N°
WHITE GOLD LEAF METALWORK WITH SAND
BLASTED "BAROQUE SHAPED" DROPS

STANDARD LAMP x 4 N°

NATURAL COLOURED PAPER
VENEER SHADE

STAINLESS STEEL ROD TO
TAKE BAYONET + CONVEY CABLE

STAINED OAK FINS
ATTACHED TO STEEL ROD

Amended

TABLE LAMP x 13 x N°

PAINTED STEEL
COVERING PLATE

These sketches were made as proposals for lighting elements within various *Homefront* schemes. There is an enormous amount of lighting products available on the market, so have a good look and find the best selection for your room.

LAYERS OF ARTIFICIAL LIGHT

When evaluating the best lighting scheme in a room, always think in terms of the three layers of light: general, accent and task lighting. The best lighting schemes will offer plenty of flexibility, so always aim to use at least three types of lighting. Blending these layers with care will create a more dynamic, stimulating atmosphere.

General or ambient light controls the general illumination of a room, playing the role of daylight. General light can include both direct and indirect (reflected) light sources. Lights in this category include central pendant lights, ceiling-mounted fittings, wall lights, downlighters, uplighters and standard lamps. I'm not a great fan of central lights and use them very rarely because I find them unflattering and inflexible and they tend to leave the corners of a room in shadow, which makes the room feel smaller. Working exceptions to this are when they are positioned over a dining table or as specific decorative features, for example, hanging in a shelving recess or with one in each corner of a room. Hang them low in a room to give it an impression of more height.

Accent lighting is directional lighting that highlights particular features. These lights can create a dramatic atmosphere in an interior, with focal points and contrasts of darkness and light. This method of lighting also serves to break up the evenness of general lighting. Examples of this type of light are halogen spotlights, table lamps with opaque shades to channel light downwards, picture lights and downlighters and uplighters with wide beams positioned near walls to wash them in light.

Task lighting is a functional light designed around specific activities, such as reading, studying, cooking or shaving. It needs to be a glare-free light that does not tire the eyes and one that ensures enough light to define close detail.

Kitchen lighting needs maximum flexibility. As well as a good general level of light, task lighting is required for specific food preparation activity. Here, downlights have been fitted on the underside of the cupboards for this purpose.

Task lighting can also add to the general illumination of a room. This light requires a bulb of at least 60 watts and should be considerably brighter than the other light sources in a room. Lights should be arranged to avoid shadows being cast in the activity area. Such lights include directional lights, such as downlighters, angled lamps and spotlights. As well as lighting an activity, task lighting has the potential to improve the dynamics of a space, create divisions within it and link items of furniture into groups.

PLANNING A LIGHTING SCHEME

A lighting scheme should be planned around the architectural features in the room and around the way it is to be used. It's also advisable to come up with a vague layout for the furniture in order to have the solid elements around which to plan the lighting scheme. The next stage is to focus on the purpose of the room and the direction in which people will be facing. This is because lights need to act as dynamic points, either to clarify activities or to draw the observer's eye. We are always instantly attracted to the brightest light source, so a stronger light can successfully draw attention to the main focal points in a space. Lighting flexibility is another essential consideration to allow for the often multi-purpose functions of modern rooms. However, beware of making your lighting system overly complex with too many competing elements to read clearly.

These accent lights create a three-dimensional focal point against this wall. Accent lighting can also be used to dramatise particular features, but in this case the lights themselves form the emphasis of the display.

You may already have a drawing of your room from planning earlier stages, but if you don't I always advise starting with a scale drawing with the furniture placement marked on it. Then add crosses in the positions where you are proposing the various light sources should be. Use other lights that you have in your home to gauge how far the light in different fittings extends and then draw pools of light on your plan. You should aim for several pools of light in different parts of the room. If you discover that there are too many pools overlapping, then adjust your plan accordingly. You need to achieve a balance between glare and blandness: too much blinding light or light with too even a distribution. Working around pools of light in this way means that you are also introducing shadows to create contrast and give more emphasis to light objects. Without the use of shadows, you risk making the space look too bland.

You will need to have decided on your lighting scheme before you start decorating. This is because you will need to plan the position of plugs, switches and wall, floor and ceiling lights so the cables are in the right position. If you are changing the main elements of your scheme, you will probably need to have surfaces re-plastered where plugs have been moved or wall and recessed lights fitted.

Particularly crucial if you have a small or awkward-size room is to try to illuminate at least three of the corners in a room, as dark corners significantly reduce the perception of a space. This trick can also be used in reverse if your space is too large and undefined – leaving dark corners will draw the parameters of the room in. Another technique for small rooms with low ceilings is to project light up with a recessed uplighter. This will wash the wall with light and draw the eye upwards in the same way as a vertical stripe. Downlighters, in contrast, can bring the height of a ceiling down because it is less well illuminated, but casting pools of light on the floor can create the impression of depth in a small room. These are all subtle cues that need to be carefully balanced around the way a room works to present a space in the most effective way.

Think, too, about the sort of style you would like your room to have and plan the lights accordingly. Even once you have selected the right lights, you still need to decide on their position. In a formal room, for example, lights will work better at the same height, with maybe a mixture of uplighters and wall lights. Or for a more relaxed, eclectic feel, use lights at different levels, while not forgetting to create a sense of visual rhythm. In a modern room with a high volume of glass surfaces or a conservatory area, the artificial light will be lost through the glass. In this situation, use a number of low-intensity lights rather than a few bright ones.

Picture lights can be tremendously effective, drawing the viewer's attention to a picture that defines the style of the room.

ON LOCATION

The dark, north-facing living room at the front of this tall 1860s' terraced house was used as a study-come-storage area. The light in the room was very grey and the outlook was towards a busy road.

The kitchen at the other side of the house had recently been extended. This room was very light with French doors at the south end and two large skylights creating maximum glare into the room in the middle of the day. This two-room brief introduced quite different problems: one not having enough light and the other with too much light and glare.

The north-facing room needed to work really hard at all levels in order to make it warmer and lighter and the measures introduced were all designed to reflect and bounce back light into the room. Wooden shelves were built for the two alcoves constructed from sturdy scaffolding planks glazed with a high-gloss varnish, with shelves built to allow the positioning of two small lights in the centre of each one (*see page 52*). A large mirror was placed opposite the window and mirror slips were fixed at an angle next to the window, again to create maximum light reflection. The walls were painted mint green, a gas-effect fire was installed in the original cast-iron fireplace and long white canvas curtains used in the window. The lighting system consists of a central pendant with the judicious use of task and accent lights in other parts of the room.

The untreated floorboards were stained brown and varnished with a high gloss to create maximum reflection of the available light.

The bright kitchen at the south end of the house was painted the same mint green (green is the warmer end of the cool part of the colour spectrum, so can work in rooms with quite different light qualities). The grey slate floor (without a high gloss) was installed to absorb more of the natural light. Because of the bright natural light that this room receives, there had also been deep pools of shadow created where the light didn't reach. The lighting scheme, therefore, needed to be as flexible and varied as possible to cater for all these conditions. Narrow shelves were constructed around each of the two roof lights where pots of ivy were placed, which will eventually grow around the windows and create a pleasant diffused light and balance the colours in the room. Fluorescent strips were also placed in each skylight to mimic the quality of natural downlighting in the latter part of the day as the daylight disappeared. Other layers of lights included wall lights, fixed and directional downlighters, ensuring there were no dark corners and no shadows in the food preparation area, a pendant light over the dining table and decorative rope lights around the base of the kitchen units. The area by the French doors had a seating area with directional downlights for reading and the doors were shielded from the bright south light with Venetian blinds.

DESIGN RULES

Both natural and artificial lights have different emphases in their spectral balance. Choose artificial lights (that tend either to have a red and yellow, or a blue and green emphasis) with a spectrum that suits the room and how you want to use it.

If we don't get enough natural light, we are vulnerable to winter lethargy. Maximise natural daylight by not blocking light from windows, using reflective surfaces and avoiding dark, matt colours.

Understand what daylight your home gets and how it changes. Generally, north- and east-facing windows require devices to maximise the quality and quantity of daylight and south- or west-facing ones benefit from devices to control light.

If windows are affected by uncomfortable glare, find ways of controlling the natural levels of sunlight.

A lighting scheme should be planned around the architectural features in the room and how it is to be used. Create a balance between glare and blandness by using a scale drawing of the room and adding the positions of the lighting elements.

Choose bulbs for artificial lighting according to the requirements of the room and the mood you would like to create: red and yellow-tinted light will create an intimate, warm mood and blue and green-tinted light will create a cooler, serene mood.

The materials used in light fittings (from transparent to opaque and reflective to matt) and the opaqueness or clarity of the bulb will dramatically affect the distribution and direction of light.

Decide on your lighting scheme before you start decorating, so you can plan the position of plugs, switches and wall, floor and ceiling lights.

In small rooms, aim to light all four corners to make the space seem bigger and use lights with vertical beams to increase the perception of height.

The best lighting schemes will offer plenty of flexibility to allow for multi-purpose functions and to create visual texture, so aim to use at least three types of lighting.

Think of lights in terms of three categories: general (for background illumination) accent (to draw attention to particular features) and task lighting (to illuminate particular activities).

3 COLOUR

Colour is a powerful tool. It has a central place at the heart of our culture and our language: the expressions 'white knight', 'green fingers', 'paint the town red' and 'blue blood' are just a few examples of how colours are used as descriptive classifications. We also link colours to emotions with expressions such as 'green with envy', 'seeing red' and 'feeling blue'. English has more words used exclusively to describe colours than any other language, 11 in fact: black, white, grey, red, orange, yellow, green, blue, purple, pink and brown (other words for colour such as aubergine, peach, terracotta and rose are associative descriptions). Yet in our homes we seem to treat colour with nervousness, the majority of us preferring magnolia and other shades of cream as paint colours on our walls above any more adventurous choices. You may know that I'm rather fond of strong, saturated colours, but all interior designers – and therefore home decorators, too – need to understand that no colour is right or wrong until it is considered alongside an interior. The distinctive shape of a room, the quality of its light and how it is to be used will point to the more effective use of particular colours over others. Getting it right will transform the room as well as the experience of those who spend time there. This chapter will explain how colour influences us and how to use colour rules to transform our homes.

THE SIGNIFICANCE OF COLOUR

Particular hues have strong symbolic meanings, but these meanings can vary enormously from culture to culture. The colour of mourning, black in Europe and America for example, is white in Asia, purple in Thailand, yellow in Egypt and Burma, red in South Africa, brown in India. Colour has often had more internationally recognised associations with particular colours symbolic of status and ownership, invariably because of the expense of manufacturing the colour. The Romans extracted the purple dye Tyrian purple from the murex snail in the Mediterranean Sea and because it was so expensive to produce, Caesar decreed that only the emperor and his household should wear purple. It was thereafter associated with authority and nobility. In more recent times, family landowners would often paint their farm buildings in certain colours to define them as theirs – a reddy orange on the Aclands' Killerton estate in Devon and a pale yellow at the Holnicote estate in Somerset, for example. Colours also act as signals: a white flag is the symbol of a truce, a yellow ribbon is a sign of support for soldiers and red means danger (although in China a red light meant 'go' until 1974!). Colour is still an important method of establishing ownership and the colours we choose in our homes are a territorial assertion, as much as a creative statement of personal taste.

We haven't always had a full palette of colours at our disposal. Indeed, until 150 years ago all dyes were drawn from natural sources in the insect and plant worlds. In 1856 a young scientist called William Perkin discovered how to make a mauve artificial dye. This led to an impressive range of dark, saturated colours becoming available such as ruby reds, mahogany browns and forest greens, which the Victorians adopted enthusiastically over the paler, more 'natural' colours to which they had been accustomed. They believed that these vibrant, rich colours gave their rooms extra importance. We are now privileged to have an astonishing range of colours from which to choose in every aspect of our lives, but maybe this in itself is a little confusing. Do we have too much choice and not enough rules? Well, although colour is often a subjective choice, the rules are there, too.

Ham House, the National Trust property in Surrey, was built in the seventeenth century and was the social centre of court life during the Restoration. The Duke's dressing room is elaborately decorated in a deep red damask wallcovering, a colour associated with privilege and royalty.

HOW THE EYE SEES COLOUR

We have already looked at the physics of how we react to light (*see page* 32) and discovered that colours are created by the nature of the light surrounding them and by how objects reflect certain wavelengths of light and absorb others. Light is made up of electromagnetic radiation and each visible colour has its own individual wavelength, or frequency. The chart below shows the wavelength measurement (measured in angstroms) of the seven colours that Sir Isaac Newton first discovered within white light in 1660 when he shone white light through a prism.

Blue, green and red are the three colours to which the 'cones' in our eyes are sensitive. We have short wavelength cones that absorb blue light, middle wavelength cones that absorb green light and long wavelength cones that absorb red light. For colours with wavelengths that fall between those of red, green and blue, combinations of the cones are stimulated to create the hues that we recognise. Because red

has a longer frequency, the eye needs to work harder to adjust to the frequency, which is why it is associated with warmth and energy. Because the frequency of green requires no adjustment on the part of the eye, it is seen is as a restful, calming colour.

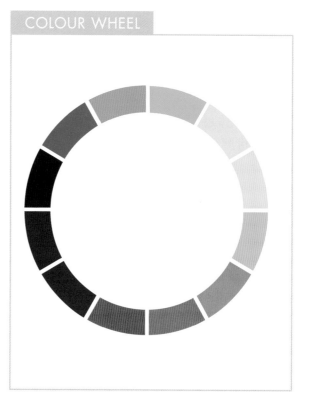

COLOUR WHEEL

COLOUR RELATIONSHIPS

A colour has three attributes: a hue (the identification of a certain type of colour), a value (how dark or light it is) and an intensity (its saturation). These three attributes are interconnected and it is impossible to change the level of one without altering the others. Each hue can be altered by mixing it with different hues. To raise the value, white is added (creating a tint) and to lower it black is added (creating a shade). Finally, to heighten the intensity of colour, more of the pure hue should be added and to lower it grey should be added.

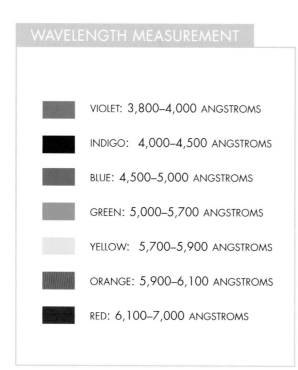

WAVELENGTH MEASUREMENT

VIOLET: 3,800–4,000 ANGSTROMS

INDIGO: 4,000–4,500 ANGSTROMS

BLUE: 4,500–5,000 ANGSTROMS

GREEN: 5,000–5,700 ANGSTROMS

YELLOW: 5,700–5,900 ANGSTROMS

ORANGE: 5,900–6,100 ANGSTROMS

RED: 6,100–7,000 ANGSTROMS

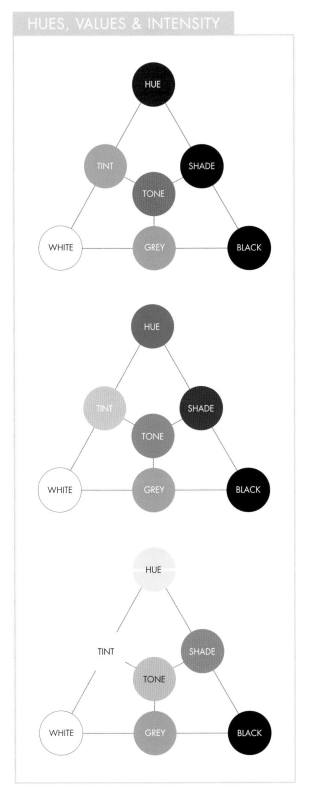

The pure hues are brighter, stronger and more energetic and the greyer tones (shades) and paler tones (tints) are subtler and therefore more restful for rooms. Grey shades and tints of particular hues can be tremendously useful to create different values and gentler shades within a chosen scheme, but beware of using too high a proportion of grey shades, as it can flatten out the pure hues and look too dull.

COLOUR MODIFICATION

It is unusual to see single colours in isolation and in interior spaces there is a constant interaction between the various colour values used. There are guidelines to help focus your choice of colours in a room (*see Colour schemes on pages* 74–75), but you should also understand how the quality of certain colours can alter when in the vicinity of other colours. When placed close to each other, complementary colours (such as blue and orange, red and green, or purple and yellow) intensify each other. This is because our visual system creates a colour's complementary and then projects it on adjacent colours, tinting them accordingly. So, because of this, pure primary colours will flatten out neutrals, a colour will look brighter if its surroundings are dark or neutral, and light and dark colour tones darken and brighten each other respectively. What happens in these cases is that the background colour will subtract, or absorb, its own hue and therefore project the hues that remain. This effect is referred to as simultaneous contrast. Although the illustrations on page 60 are showing small squares enclosed by larger squares of colour, which heightens the effect of simultaneous contrast, just the same effect is created with adjacent colours and, indeed, any colours in juxtaposition that take up a large enough area to register as a colour.

design **RULES**

COLOUR INTERACTION

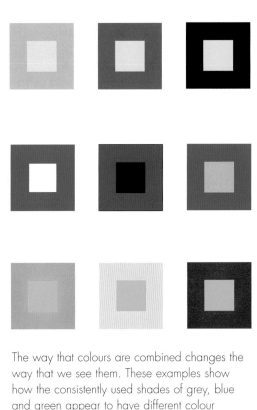

The way that colours are combined changes the way that we see them. These examples show how the consistently used shades of grey, blue and green appear to have different colour qualities according to the colours used nearby.

This optical illusion means that colour hues that we use in our homes can be pushed in different directions. So, a turquoise sofa in front of an orange wall will mean that one intensifies the colours of the other, whereas a turquoise sofa in front of an olive green wall will mean that the turquoise colour will appear to be tinted slightly with red (the complementary of green), giving the impression of a more purple blue. Or, a pair of honey-coloured silk curtains on a pale grey wall will appear darker than if the wall was painted a navy blue – this is because the 'light' wall takes the impact away from the light colour of the curtains whereas a darker wall will accentuate it.

COLOURS THAT ADVANCE AND RECEDE

Because of the different wavelengths that colours contain (*see How the eye sees colour on page* 58), those towards the red end of the spectrum (red, orange and yellow) with longer wavelengths tend to 'advance' towards the observer. Those towards the violet end of the spectrum (violet, indigo, blue and green) with shorter wavelengths tend to 'recede' away from the observer. It is believed that this colour phenomenon may be because of colour associations with the physical world, with red representing the close warmth of fire and blue the distant sky, water or ice. This means that a chosen colour can make a surface or an object look further away or closer to the point of vision. How strongly it will advance or recede depends on its intensity, so the purer a colour the more advancing qualities it has (such as pillar-box red) and the more 'combined' a colour when mixed with other hues, then the more these qualities will be lessened (such as earth brown).

Darker colours (of any hue) also advance and make surfaces seem smaller, and lighter colours recede and make surfaces seem larger. This is because of their absorption and reflection qualities. White will reflect the maximum amount of light off a surface, so a pale orange or a pale blue (tints of the pure hue) which have significant quantities of white in them will make more light reflect off them. Pure black will dramatically absorb light, and so a dark orange or a dark blue (shades of the pure hue) will have black in them, which means that more light is absorbed. So, the actual advancing or receding impact of a colour will depend on the exact hue, intensity and saturation that is used. A dark blue wall will appear closer than a pale pink one and a pale orange could have so much white in it that it acts as a colour that pushes back the walls of a room rather than enclosing them. This advancing and receding colour rule applies equally to furniture and furnishings, so a scarlet chair will appear as larger than a pale blue one, so you can change covers where you want to draw attention towards, or away from, furnishing elements.

To put this into practice in a room with a low ceiling, paint a cool, light, low-contrast colour (one that is lighter than the walls) such as white, light blue, pale grey or lilac above the picture rail of a room and across the ceiling to make the ceiling feel higher. Don't forget that vertical stripes will also enhance the height of a room (*see Pattern and illusion on pages* 98–99). In reverse, for a room with an awkwardly high ceiling, use a darker or more intense colour on the ceiling, above the picture rail (if there is no picture rail, then create one, as was done with the location on pages 148–152). You can also paint features such as coving and ceiling roses in a lighter colour, again bringing them closer to the viewer.

In order to make a small room seem larger and dissipate any feeling of claustrophobia, then choose pale, receding colours for the walls, windows and ceiling. The nearer the colour is to white, then the more light it will bounce around the room and the larger the space will seem. Painting the skirting boards the same colour as the carpet or flooring will also help give the impression that the floor is larger and wider. In an uncomfortably large room, paint the walls a warm, dark colour, such as aubergine or burnt orange, to absorb the light and make the walls seem closer, giving the room a more cosy, intimate atmosphere. Remember that really dark colours are only advisable in a room with a high ceiling that gets a significant amount of natural light.

This colour device can also be used in a room that needs more character, maybe one that is too formulaic and square. In this case, paint one of the walls a lighter or darker shade than the others which will alter the perceived proportions of the room. Or in a very narrow room or passageway, use a strong, warm colour on the

This pale blue is a classic receding colour – because we associate it with the tones of the sky above us, the walls appear to be further away. Although this shade is less effective than white in this respect, white walls can often be stark and unwelcoming.

narrow walls to make them seem closer and the room squarer. This illusion can be further emphasised by the use of a dramatic piece of furniture or artwork against the wall with the strong colour distracting the eye still further from the narrow proportions of the space.

The fact that certain colours 'advance' and certain colours 'recede' registers unconsciously with our knowledge of perspective. Leonardo da Vinci developed the idea that pale, shadowy, low-contrast colours in the background of a painting, midway colour values in the middle

COLOUR WHEEL

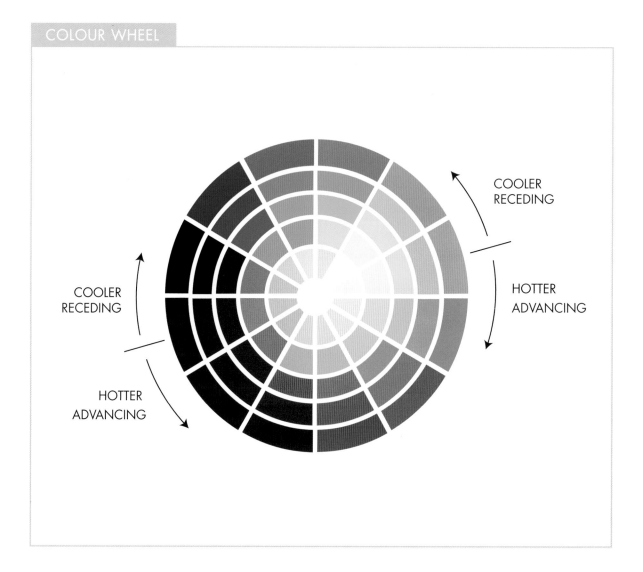

COOLER
RECEDING

HOTTER
ADVANCING

COOLER
RECEDING

HOTTER
ADVANCING

distance and more saturated, glowing colours in the foreground gave a greater impression of depth within a two-dimensional work. It is because of the association of the distant blue sky that we think that a pale blue wall is further away (colours turn blue as they become more distant because of the scattering of light) and it is the higher frequency and energetic activity of orange and red that makes these colours seem closer.

Remember that the intensity of colours will also vary according to how near or far away they are. Any hue will appear brighter when close to

the viewer than when far away. More saturated and darker colours will be less dominating when used in large spaces than in small rooms. Any colour will also have more power and visual dominance when it covers a large surface. This is why paint colour chips can be misleading and why it is good to use sample pots to paint larger areas of a given colour on your wall to give you a realistic idea of its impact. The other tip is to remember the proportion of the room you are decorating: if it is big and high, then the darker your chosen colour will appear.

These four examples show the ways that advancing and receding colours can be used to alter the perceived dimensions of a room: the top left shows how to make a room feel warm and bring down a ceiling that is too high; the top right shows how to make a room feel intimate and cosy by using a saturated, advancing colour; the bottom right shows a receding colour to make a small room feel larger; and the bottom left shows a long narrow room with advancing colours used on the narrow ends to bring the walls forward and boards or striped carpeting used across the narrow length to extend the perceived width.

Top: Every part of the world has distinctive light qualities that govern its use of colour. In places near the equator such as Morocco, cooler colours such as blue and white are used to reflect light, and often more vivid hues are used to combat the washing out of colours by the sunlight. Above: In the UK and in Scandinavia the colour schemes tend to be more knocked back, to fit around the cooler temperatures and varied light levels.

COLOURS IN DIFFERENT LIGHTS

Colours take on a different appearance within different climates because of the varying qualities and strength of sunlight. Individual parts of the world are known for colour schemes that suit the conditions: the Indian continent or hot, desert regions, for example, are associated with intense saturated colour hues heightened by the high levels of sunshine, or white colours that reflect the natural light. Scandinavia and the UK, however, are both associated with cool colours more sympathetic to the overcast northern climate and that maximise natural light and space in small rooms. This is why replicating colour schemes inspired by a holiday in Morocco can be a mistake in grey, damp Britain, where the hues are subdued by the weaker natural light and therefore act as darkening agents in our homes.

These geographical differences in light illustrate how dramatically the value of a colour can be changed by the light around it. At a more local level, the individual daylight qualities in a room in the UK can guide you towards the use of certain colours over others. First of all, consider what direction your windows face (*see Assessing your quality of light and how it changes on page 36–37*). For east-facing windows that get the early morning sun, subtle, warm colours such as yellow or muted orange will enhance the warmth of the sun and still provide a warm glow as the day progresses and the sun moves away. West light can benefit from a cool scheme of light values in colours ranging from blues to violets. If the east- or west-facing room is used mainly in the morning, decorate it in the same way as you would a south-facing room or a room to the west as if it were facing north. The same is true in reverse if the room is mainly used in the evening. If the room is used all day, a balance of warm and cold colours should complement the changing light. One trick that

I've used in east- and west-facing rooms is to have reversible cushions, throws and blinds with contrasting colours on each side. One side should be in a colour designed to maximise indirect light (in cream or other pale, neutral colours) and the other with warmer colours providing a comforting glow when there is direct sunlight or for later in the evening in artificial lighting.

For south-facing windows with strong light levels, you have the most flexibility with your colour choice. Cool mid-tones and neutrals can work well, because southern light will make any colours seem lighter and more saturated. Or, if your south-facing room has uncomfortably strong levels of light, try using dark and unsaturated colours to absorb more light and help balance glare. For north-facing rooms, always the coldest rooms with the least available sunlight, warm colours give them a more welcoming quality (*see* On location *on pages 78-82* where tangerine orange was used on all four walls). If light and saturated colours are used in warm colours, then more light is reflected into the room.

The same differences are perceived between natural light and artificial lighting. Natural light will always give a colour more intensity because it is nearest to pure white light. So, a warm light such as tungsten will make warm colours such as red and yellow appear warmer, and cooler colours such as blue and green even cooler; whereas a colder light such as fluorescent will heighten the effect of cool colours and undermine the strength of warm colours. The contrast between the cool white fluorescent lighting in retail stores and the incandescent sources used in the home can mean that a purchase appears quite a different colour at home than in the shop, an illusion called metamerism. The value of a colour can also be heightened or reduced through the intensity of the light: lowering the light level will darken a colour and neutralise its hue and raising it will lighten the colour and enhance its intensity. Beware though, as high levels of light can also wash out colours. All this shows how our visual understanding of colour is a sensation created through our eyes' reaction to light rather than being a physical property of a given object.

ARTIFICIAL LIGHT & COLOUR

Daylight colours (white light)	Incandescent source (yellow white light)	Low-voltage halogen (warm bright light)	Fluorescent (blue white light)
red	red orange	bright red	dull red
yellow	yellow orange	intense yellow	green yellow
green	blue green	yellow green	blue green
blue	blue	green blue	bright blue
white	white	off white	white

THE PSYCHOLOGY OF COLOUR

Apart from the proven scientific qualities of colour, different colour shades can also have powerful psychological influences. The ancient mystics in China believed that each person has a distinctive aura that changes colour to correspond to their current emotional state. Colour healing is still practised today and treats seven energy centres or 'chakras' (represented by different parts of the body) with particular colours to address mental or emotional imbalances. Colour healers believe that colours have individual energies and, curiously, the basis of this spiritual belief is not in conflict with the scientific explanation of colour having different wavelengths.

Research into the physiological effects of colour has shown definite changes in human heart rate and brain activity when enclosed in rooms of different colours, with the red and orange end of the spectrum proving to be more stimulating and the blue and green end of the spectrum more calming. However, such studies have shown that these effects tend to be short-lived, with the body soon adjusting to the surrounding colour. The saturation of a colour seems to have more impact than the actual colour, so intense colours are more arousing and low-intensity colours more relaxing, no matter what the hue. For this reason, it seems fair to assume that the most effective way of using your choice of hue to influence people in your home may be to use appropriate value colours in entranceways, to create an effective short-term visual impact for visitors.

Despite this far from definitive conclusion, it should be recognised that colour continues to be used successfully in interiors to regulate the mood of those spending time there. Fast-food restaurants tend to use shades of red, orange and yellow, longer wavelength colours that are all believed to make you eat more. The paint manufacturer Farrow & Ball, who produce 'historic' paint colours specially developed for National Trust properties, have a deep red shade called Eating Room Red, a colour that was popular in the middle of the nineteenth century. Casinos also use red, as it imitates the colour of evening light and makes you less aware of the passing of time. There is also a corporation in Japan designing rooms around the temperaments of those living in them. They have worked particularly with hyperactive or inhibited children, typically treating the former type with calming, low-contrast colours; the latter type with saturated warm colours. Early studies even indicate that particular colours can increase or reduce productivity in the workplace. One study in the 1970s painted the whole of the working environment yellow and this was found to considerably reduce productivity, with the pervading yellow causing the eye to create distracting negative after-images of its complementary, purple. The colour blue is associated with calm and can be a powerful atmosphere-creator too, often used in prisons to reduce stress. Hospitals also tend to use white and other cool colours such as blue to create a healing, restful environment. It has been shown that people feel considerably warmer in red and orange rooms, and colder in violet, blue and green rooms, even when the temperatures are equivalent.

Opposite: Hot colours, such as red, pink and orange, are known to keep the brain more active and there are those who conclude that this makes them inappropriate for use in relaxing rooms such as bedrooms and bathrooms. But this does depend on the exact shade used; crimson or acid orange will be far more stimulating than pale orange or watery pink, for example. There is also the option to use such strong colours, but introduce other colours to balance out their impact. In this kitchen design proposal for *Homefront*, a scheme of pink, grey and white was used, with the grey and white making the pink a dominant highlight rather than the main emphasis.

PERSONAL COLOUR PREFERENCES

Despite all these behavioural associations, we should avoid becoming so regulated by 'colour rules' that we forget that each person has their own likes and dislikes that may differ from the theories of science and psychology. Many of these are linked to our culture as well as our upbringing and personal history. We might have unpleasant associations with certain colours from our childhood that thereafter create negative feelings when we encounter them. It also seems that most of us naturally prefer colours that complement our skin type, hair and eye colour and invariably choose such tones for our homes and our clothes. There are also colour theories that link particular combinations of colours with individual personality types.

There are reliable development patterns to do with colour preferences. Vision develops very fast in children: new-born babies are sensitive to light and dark, two-week old babies respond to red and green and at two months they respond to blue and yellow (the larger neurons required for red and green vision start developing earlier than the blue and yellow ones). At four months, they show a definite preference for red and blue, and red is invariably the first colour in a child's vocabulary. Children of four and five tend to prefer brighter, saturated colours, with preferences for shorter wavelength colours such as blue and green developing later, sometimes only at adolescence. A study of 21,000 adults in the West showed that blue was the favourite colour, followed by red, green and violet with yellow and white right at the bottom (whites and yellows are, however, more favoured in Asia).

COLOUR ASSOCIATIONS

Having assessed how colours can have strong psychological triggers, there now follows an individual analysis of the ways that different colours can affect us both mentally and physically and how we might start to make decisions about where to use them in our homes. Much of this information is linked to alternative philosophies such as colour healing and associations with colour that have been made over the centuries rather than having been scientifically proven. Although this may have less factual weight, it's all food for thought in the great colour debate.

RED

This is the longest wavelength colour and the furthest from both black and white. It has a powerful resonance and it is usually the first colour word that children will use. In history, red has been linked to royalty and victory and protection, with some Australian aborigines painting their weapons red to give them magic powers. Less positively, it is also associated with anger, danger, blood, fire and violence. Red light will stimulate human heart function and can build up red blood cells in the body and can also help with depression. It is a stimulating, energetic, passionate colour that can be used to create an atmosphere of excitement and intensity. Because it induces appetite, it can be a good colour to use in dining rooms. It is also flattering to the skin, so can be effective in rooms used for entertaining. It is a strong advancing colour, so can reduce the apparent proportions of a room or bring a single wall or object further forward. It is supposed to stimulate brain activity, but is also believed to be tiring over long periods. Some people advise against the use of red in a bedroom or bathroom because of its stimulating qualities, but I know that red can be a wonderful atmosphere-inducer in both these rooms: it all depends on the personality of the owners and the exact shade that is used. Pillar-box red is just one of a wide spectrum of hues: choose from other shades such as plum red, Elizabethan red, raspberry, cranberry, russet, oxblood, burgundy, crimson, carmine, magenta, scarlet and wine.

Many designers would not advise the use of strong saturated colours such as this deep red in rooms used for relaxation and repose. I would never dismiss the use of a colour based on how the room is used; in this example the deep red shade gives a strong identity to the bathroom and would give a cosy, enclosing feeling when reclining in the bath.

The use of colour in this room and stairwell is full of feminine eccentricity. The cerise pink walls in the understair area create a comfortable, welcoming seating area and the pink theme recurs up the stairs and within other furnishing details.

PINK

Pink is a softer version, or a tint, of pure red. Formed by adding white to red, it is the gentler side of red, so that while red is passionate and fiery, pink is swooning and romantic, associated with little girls and femininity. It is also associated with innocence, purity and good health (think of 'in the pink') – as well as tasteful men's suits! Pink can be playful, tender, flirtatious and alluring. A pink shade will act as a muscle relaxant and will also unwind tense emotions. It is therefore good for comfort and healing and can have a calming effect in a room, reducing violent outbursts in difficult children. The intensity of the colour will make a dramatic difference to the psychological effect. Choose from shades such as flamingo, coral, salmon, rose, fuchsia and pastel pink.

ORANGE

Orange is next to red on the spectrum and has the same energetic, advancing qualities in a room, although its lower wavelength means that it is slightly less intense. But this can be a real advantage: orange provides a friendly, flexible, lively colour for increasing warmth and activity and will give a palpable warming glow to north- and east-facing rooms. Like red, it is an appetite stimulant and in colour therapy it is believed to bolster the immune system, increase sexual potency and help with digestive ailments. This stimulating colour is also said to combat depression and promote self-esteem. Remember all the available hues of orange: among them peach, cinnamon, tangerine, apricot, amber, pumpkin, terracotta and vermilion.

The orange tint and highlights within this living space give a warm glow to the room, while the pale tone of the walls also allows maximum definition of space.

YELLOW

This colour has a strong association with springtime sunlight, and therefore with new beginnings, well-being and optimism. It is an uplifting and cheerful colour that can warm any north-facing room, but its shades have very different effects: lighter yellows endow a space with light and freedom, but dark yellows can dominate and overpower a space. Remember, too, that cool yellows such as lemon yellow can give a green cast in the British climate. Yellow is seen as the colour of the intellect and is supposed to make your brain function more effectively, so try yellow in a study or office space. This colour is often used successfully in dining and entertainment spaces where a bright mood is required. It is used in colour healing to help dermatitis and other skin problems. Goethe classified yellow as the most positive colour: the closest to pure light and the opposite of melancholic blue. It is believed to improve memory and judgement and to promote optimism. Think of the full range of yellows, including mustard, saffron, lemon, ochre, corn and canary yellow.

GREEN

Although in the Middle Ages, green was seen as an evil colour, it now has a secure status as the colour of nature, representing growth, new life and harmony. Forests, trees, grass, mosses, pears, apples, melons and limes are all products of nature that engender distinctive shades of green. The wavelength of the colour green is the one that the brain has to make least effort to adapt to and this is why it is a calming, comforting, healing, non-aggressive colour. In colour therapy, green is used to balance the heart, the lungs and the blood circulation, regulate breathing patterns, stimulate growth and healing and reduce stress. The more saturated greens such as apple and lime green have warmer, energising qualities whereas darker shades such as olive and forest green have a more serious, subdued atmosphere and the paler tints the most receding and restful qualities. Other shades include bottle green, pea green, lichen, sage, teal, chartreuse and emerald.

Green, of whatever hue, has a gentle, calming effect on an interior. This is because its wavelengths are easily adjusted to by the human visual system.

71

The colour blue is always associated with calming, relaxing qualities, and yet the more saturated range of blue shades has a resonant quality that can give real definition to a room.

BLUE

Our strongest association with blue is the sky and the sea – even in ancient Rome and Greece sky blue was the colour of Jupiter and Zeus. Because it is most often seen in the far distance, it is the most powerful colour to use to push back the walls in a room and maximise the feeling of space. Goethe classified blue as the most negative colour and the closest hue in the spectrum to black. The lapis lazuli blue pigment used in the Middle Ages had a higher value than gold and this was the reason that it was used to represent the Virgin Mary. It has associations with coolness, protection and formality while also setting a peaceful atmosphere for spiritual escape and dreaming. In colour healing, blue is used to stimulate healing, relieve pain and bring down blood pressure. It is supposed to encourage deep and peaceful sleep in bedrooms. In its darker shades, blue can give elegance to a formal reception room and its lighter tints will give a lightweight, calming background to any room. Shades of blue include cornflower, navy, aquamarine, ultramarine, oxford, sky, cyan, indigo, azure, cobalt and cerulean.

VIOLET/PURPLE

These hues are a unique mixture of red and blue, an uncertain colour mixture of positive and negative hues that Goethe considered to be disturbing. The range of hues within this band are majestic, refined, dignified colours. They are believed to have spiritual healing qualities and in psychology violet is used to help mental equilibrium by calming patients suffering from paranoia. These are supposed to be colours that inspire the imagination: Leonardo da Vinci thought that meditation was ten times as effective in a purple light. Purple dyes were developed by the Romans using a species of Mediterranean snail and were worn by Roman emperors, and by members of the monarchy and aristocracy ever since, to reinforce their privileged status. Purples have always had religious significance, too, with violet associated with the Passion of Christ. At their most dark and dramatic, violet-purple hues can be used to create theatrical environments, cocooned retreats away from modern life and at their most conventional paler lilacs and violets provide excellent restful background colours. Choose from aubergine, plum, lavender, maroon, violet, orchid and lilac to feather your nest in purple.

Purple has a real meditative quality, as well as all the calming qualities of its close neighbour, blue.

White will create maximum reflection of natural light and so is often a good choice for dark or awkwardly shaped rooms. The classic white interior has a stylistic quality all of its own, in this case a combination of monastic purity and modern comforts.

BROWN

The spectrum of this colour is very wide: tints of brown such as mushroom or biscuit can be cool and shades of brown such as cocoa or chocolate can be warm. With colours associated with the earth, wood, lichen and other natural materials, it has a practical, wholesome character that epitomises the forces of nature as well as stability, comfort and the warmth of home. Its warmer cousins such as golden brown and tan can stimulate the appetite. Despite its earthy dependability, brown can also have a rich, elegant sophistication. It combines well with rich colours, such as purples and golds, or with lighter tints of itself, such as beige and cream. The many brown hues available include chocolate, golden brown, tan, oyster, taupe, mushroom, biscuit, cocoa, sand, beige and cream.

WHITE

The colour white is in fact a non-colour, a combination of all the colours of the spectrum. White is the colour of purity and of heavenly figures and is also associated with youth, reverence and humility and is believed to relieve pain. It is frequently used in the architecture of hot climates, such as Mediterranean countries, because of its effective reflective qualities. White has the greatest potential of any colour to make the walls of a room recede and although it can have great intensity, it can also be a stark, soulless choice in large or cold rooms. Inuits, amazingly, have over 17 words for white used to describe the various qualities of snow and ice: our more limited references include ivory and alabaster.

GREY/SILVER

Grey is a neutral shade, a halfway point between white and black. It has cool, cloudy qualities that can be both conservative and moody. It is a purging colour associated with peace, calm and uncertainty. Silver has the same cool, noble qualities as grey, but is more animated and spiritual. Grey and silver combine effectively with other cool shades such as blue or green. Choose from stone, concrete, steel, granite and slate.

BLACK

Not strictly a colour and representing an absence of light, black can be empty and oppressive when used on large areas, also making a room feel much smaller than it is. Seen as formal, dignified and austere, it also carries a sense of protection and mystery. There are those who believe that black can be used to restrain personal development or to block change. Black in the interior can be dramatic and expressive when used as accents to illuminate colour schemes, integrated with bright colours, splashes of colour or with neutral shades, for example. Blacks include ebony, sable, midnight and raven.

design **RULES**

COLOUR SCHEMES

Colour is a complex issue, as we have seen, with often intricate scientific and psychological theories. Both sets of theories can be extended into interior colour schemes: some designers will work around theories of feng shui, colour healing or behavioural associations with colour, while others refer constantly to the colour wheel, extending the science that establishes how colours combine most effectively into their interior designs. It is possible to divide colour schemes based on the colour wheel into classifications such as monochromatic, complementary, triadic, tetradic, even split and double complementary schemes, terms that personally I find take the excitement out of the design process. My approach to colour involves close references to these elements, but I prefer to tune into a passionate, personal reaction that is not distracted by formula. I like to create rooms for individuals and to create colour schemes that respond to their qualities and preferences. Probably, as a homeowner reading this, it is likely that this is your inspiration, too. So, don't let your concern about a small window and the relative wavelength of colours override the fact that you would love to have a cerise-pink study; don't obsess about making a small room bigger by using pale blue paint on the walls if what you really want is to create a cosy, warm nest with shades of rust and deep orange; and, certainly, don't paint your spare room scarlet just to keep your less popular guests awake at night. It is all about balancing what you know about colour and making it relevant to you.

I believe that the most successful colour schemes are based on analagous hues, or what I call colour families. This means picking three or more colours that are adjacent to each other on the colour wheel and using them as the

This scheme draws from the red/orange side of the colour spectrum. Highlights of white lift the overall combination of warm, saturated colours.

theme in a room, with one as the dominant hue. The colour wheel on page 62, illustrating 12 colour hues in the centre, tints of the hue moving inwards and shades of the hue moving outwards, shows the enormous range and depth of colour options that are available following the colour-family rule.

So, in a spacious north-facing room with a grey light, you might choose earth brown, golden brown, orange and russet with accents of plum and maroon. In a small room with a cold light you could opt for a part of the colour wheel that introduces elements of warmth, but that also helps to make the walls recede. Think of tints of aquamarine, ultramarine, olive, emerald and lime with accents of the warmer pure hues and golden browns or deep reds (both opposite this colour family on the colour wheel) to give more warmth. For a more neutral scheme in a sunny

room, you could choose cream, beige, taupe, honey and yellow with accents of mocca and chocolate brown.

The choices are endless, and the exact proportions of each colour can be balanced so that the dominant ones (it is always better to have a single, dominant hue) are either those that you adore or those that work hard to make the room work better. Always avoid using a colour in just one place: repeating colour elements harmonise the space and make each one read more strongly whereas an incidental splash of a colour will look like a mistake. Don't limit yourself to the 12 colours and their light and dark variations shown in this particular wheel, as there are many other alternatives. Try collecting paint charts that are often published in colour families as a visual guide: cut them out and create your own colour family to apply to any room in your home.

Visual contrast is often best judged by half closing your eyes in search of a pleasing balance between light, midway and dark shades.

VISUAL CONTRAST

Choosing a colour scheme for a room requires the right balance of colour values in the same way as a painting or a textile design. As well as the exact colour scheme, the individual qualities of the colours and how they can distort other nearby colours (*see Colour modification on pages* 59–60), they should also be chromatically and tonally balanced. This means achieving a harmonious balance between neutral, midway and intense colour and between the lights and darks within a space.

Use opposites of light and dark to spice up the visual texture of a scheme: too much dark colour can be depressing and dominating and too much light colour can be stark and bland. If one is the dominant hue, use highlights of the other to give drama and vivacity to the scheme. The visual contrast trick is also helpful in order to distinguish elements. Having an emerald green chair in front of an emerald green wall will mean that the shape of the chair will be lost in the background wall colour. However, having a lime green chair in front of the emerald green wall keeps the relationship within the same colour family (*see Colour schemes on pages* 74–75) but makes the chair more prominent. Using the same

principle, less attractive features such as pipework, radiators or a dominating chimney breast can be painted in the same shade as the walls to help them blend into the background.

However, this balance of colours and tones is also about overall composition. Some designers think of a room as a natural landscape, imitating the balance of tones from floor to ceiling from earthy browns and dark tones to mid-distance greens and mid tones to pale blues, white and light tones on the ceiling. In principle, it is advisable to use different levels of light and dark values, with middle values to provide pathways between them. In a room where light needs to be maximised, use large areas of light colour values and balance these with darker highlights. In a room where light needs to be controlled, use a mid- or dark-value colour as the main background and use lighter colours as highlights.

This balance of saturation and lightness and darkness will also emphasise (or de-emphasise) the scale of the furnishing elements in your room. If you have a bulky mahogany dressing table that you can't possibly get rid of, and which is actually far too big for your bedroom, then paint the wall behind it in a similar colour and use lighter and brighter colours as accents on the bed or elsewhere in the room to distract the eye. Or if you want to draw attention away from an awkward architectural feature, then cover seating elsewhere in blocks of strong, warm colour that will instantly draw the eye, or create a 'feature wall' (*see Pattern and illusion on pages* 100–101) away from the unsightly element. Alternatively, and I believe there should always be room for this, if you prefer to be more spontaneous about colours and have confidence in your own judgement, think about your room as a harmony of colour and mix the elements intuitively to please your own eye, adjusting them to get the right balance.

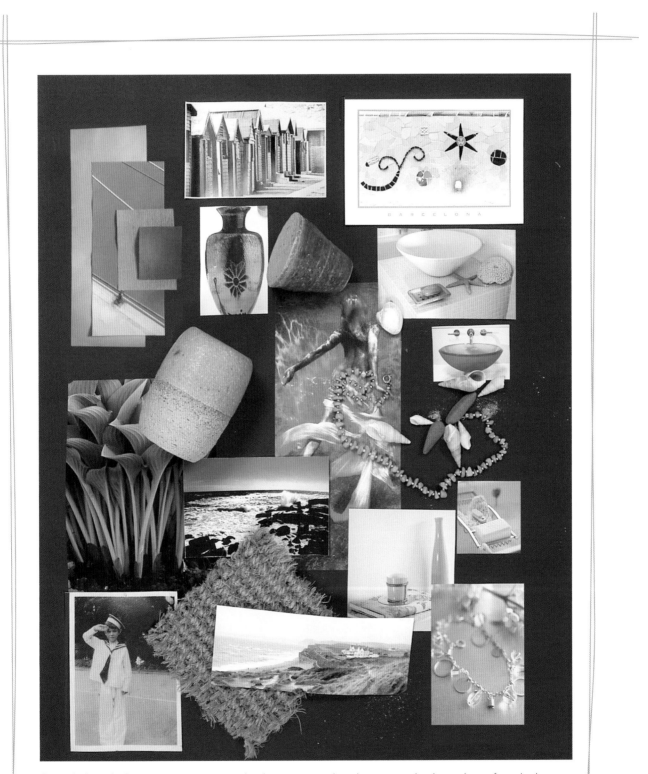

This style board of maritime inspiration and colours was used as the proposed colour scheme for a bathroom.

ON LOCATION

This room, previously used as a combined dining room and sitting room, has beautiful Victorian features – a wide, six-panelled door and an elaborate ceiling rose and cornices. It had been decorated in a textured, cream wallpaper and an oatmeal coloured carpet with neutral window-length curtains, a central pendant and a few haphazard spotlights and wall lights. Because of the dual purpose of the room – sitting and dining – there lacked a central focus, a *raison d'être*. As the room is north-facing, the neutral colours and the contrast between them and the dark, heavy pieces of furniture made it feel really cold, with a greenish light reflected from the grass outside. There was a real miscellany of colours, but none of them fitted within an overall scheme.

The most important challenge was to address the quality of the cold north light in the room. First of all, a new dark gloss wood fireplace was installed with a coal-effect fire to give a sense of balance to the chimney breast and to create a strong focal point. The room was then painted tangerine, a hot colour that bounces warm light into the room, making it welcoming and inviting. The tangerine also tints the available daylight a happier shade and compensates for the green light that bounces off the lawn outside, which turned the previous shade a bilious green. So much about the use of colour is psychological: apparently people always feel warmer in rooms painted in hot colours such as orange as opposed to cooler colours such as blue, even when the temperature is the same. This colour has 'advancing' qualities, making the walls seem closer, which worked well here as the room has generous proportions. Such warm colours also help to combat cold light, making the space more intimate, cosy and welcoming. The skirting, ceiling and cornices were painted an ivory colour (always avoid combining brilliant white with hot colours, as it can look too stark a contrast). The ceiling rose was painted with a scumble glaze to draw it out as a prominent feature.

The louvered windows were changed to plain ones that fitted with the period of the house and they were dressed with a pelmet and glazed cotton and linen curtains lined with aubergine to give some deeper colour highlights (*see pages 80–81*). A textured carpet in a warm honey colour was laid and the native African textile, which had been prominent in the room, was framed in dark wood – in combination with the orange colour scheme, this creates more richness and warmth. The dining table was placed in front of the window, to capture immediate attention when entering the room and a sofa placed next to the wall behind the door with a collection of ethnic artefacts, a comfortable seating area that didn't interrupt the main focus of the room. The fruity, sumptuous colours in this space are all drawn from the same colour family – the hot section of the colour wheel. All the accessories follow this theme: aubergine, pomegranate, deep red, ruby, apricot, autumnal orange with accents of green to spice it up and keep the eye moving around the room. Walking into the room is like being enveloped by a welcoming, orange glow, a heightened sensory experience created through the use of hot colours to combat the cold light.

DESIGN RULES

Colour has three attributes: a hue (the identification of a certain type of colour), a value (how dark or light it is) and an intensity (its saturation).

The shape of a room, the quality of its light and how it is to be used will point to the more effective use of particular colours over others.

Colours towards the red end of the spectrum with longer wavelengths tend to 'advance' towards the observer. Those towards the violet end of the spectrum with shorter wavelengths tend to 'recede' away from the observer.

Colours can be drastically affected by colours surrounding them; this is because the eye tints a colour with the complementary of an adjacent colour. This needs to be borne in mind when planning colour juxtapositions.

Colours take on individual qualities in different climates, because of the various levels and quality of sunlight. The grey UK climate suits cooler, lighter colours that maximise natural light and space.

Looking at an individual colour in natural light and then artificial light will alter its quality depending on the type of artificial lighting used.

Colour can be used successfully in the interior to regulate the mood of those spending time there.

We all have personal associations with colour that affect how we feel about them. Colours are also believed to have strong healing powers and are often used to treat physical illness or mental imbalances.

When selecting colour schemes, choose analogous hues, or colour families (three or more colours that are adjacent to each other on the colour wheel). Use one colour as the dominant hue and the others as accent colours.

Always try to achieve a harmonious balance between neutral, midway and intense colour and between the lights and darks within a space.

The purer a colour the more advancing qualities it has, and the more 'combined' a colour the more these qualities will be lessened. Equally, the paler a colour the more it will recede and the darker a colour the more it will advance.

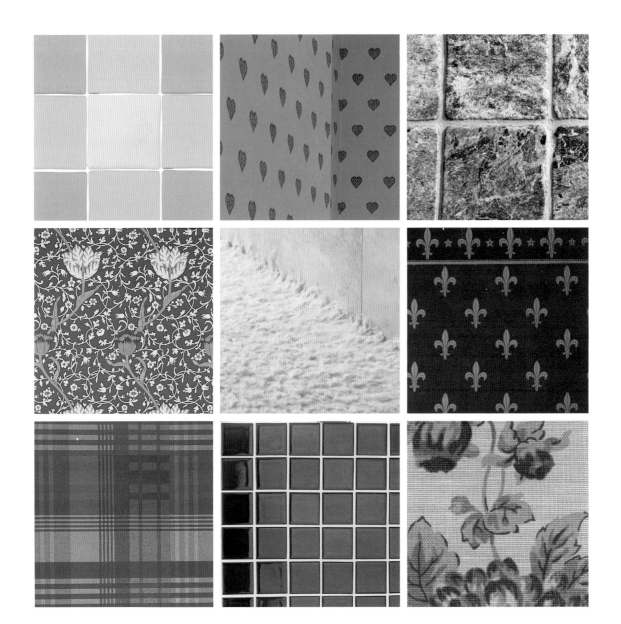

TEXTURE & PATTERN

Using decorative wallcoverings can be a simple and effective way of establishing a particular style in a room. Here, the bedroom is softened by the use of an organic wallpaper design that sets a gentle, nostalgic tone.

You may be guilty of thinking that the use of texture and pattern in an interior is a decorative afterthought, involving indulgent shopping trips to buy wallcoverings, curtains and carpets to achieve the final dressing of a room and 'finish it off' to perfection. Let me correct you here. Texture and pattern both have a major role in creating the right atmosphere in a room. They endorse and complement all the decisions you've so far made about space, light and colour. Both elements also have strong psychological connections, evoking personal memories and associations, both pleasant and disturbing, so can also be tremendously evocative. Remember that texture and pattern should not just be about embellishing a room to make it pretty, but should have an essential role in creating a meaningful three-dimensional space that follows the cues of design, science and psychology to make the interior experience more rewarding and more effective.

Our perception is roundly informed by all the 'designed' elements of an interior. Yet, texture and pattern are often the first things that we encounter in a room, or rather the first things that our brains are stimulated by. Our reaction to both involves primeval responses, orientated around survival techniques and the ability to correctly interpret our environment. The tactile quality of a surface informs us about whether it is rough or smooth, comfortable or prickly, and therefore safe or dangerous to touch or sit on. As for pattern, we already know that our eyes see the world in two dimensions and our brain translates what the eyes see into three dimensions; pattern is another major cue that defines our understanding of space and depth.

A fleur-de-lis wallpaper is one of the bestselling British wallpapers of all time. Representative of the heraldic use of pattern in the interior, it is a classic design motif that has been constantly reinvented.

Different textures have always been used to represent hardship or comfort. Monks often used to wear hair undershirts to cause intentional physical discomfort, as a constant reminder to them that sensual pleasure should be secondary to the love of God. Basic fabric textures such as hessian, canvas, woven reeds, and natural materials such as leather, stone, wood, brick and grasses kept our early ancestors in touch with the natural cycles of the earth. But because of the connection with those who can't afford better, such materials have also been associated with the unsophisticated, the primitive and the uncultured. This distinction is less apparent today in an age where we fashionably value the honesty of natural textures and surfaces. In previous centuries, though, the use of expensive, luxurious materials such as brilliantly coloured silks, damasks and velvets represented wealth, social status and refined taste and were used unashamedly in the domestic interior to assert this message. Pattern, too, has been used since the beginning of recorded history in paintings, frescoes, murals, tapestries, rugs, tiles and textiles. With purposes ranging from ceremonial, religious and symbolic to those that establish the owner's taste and family status, there is no doubt that the culture of pattern is a deeply ingrained one, and not merely rooted in a desire to decorate.

We now have an immense range of textures and patterns available to us, from our own history, from international sources and from currently evolving fashions. But how can we harness these resources sensibly as part of our domestic environment? Here are some guidelines to point the way.

design **RULES**

TEXTURE PSYCHOLOGY

Understanding the tactile quality of the objects that surround us gives us the information to interpret our world in three-dimensions and behave accordingly. As young as four months and constantly between six and 18 months, infants explore the world by straining for and grasping objects in their environment – an effective investigative technique that teaches them about the distinctive surface qualities of different objects within the strange three-dimensional world they find themselves in.

Whilst touch informs an understanding of texture, vision also serves to warn us about how an object might feel when touched – even babies as young as four months have expectations about how heavy an object might be. Our visual understanding of texture becomes so well developed that we can interpret textures without actually touching them. At first sight, we understand the sensuous rich pile of a velvet surface or how a knobbly, moss-ingrained tree trunk will feel. The accumulation of sensory experience enables us to make connections between what we see and what we already know.

TEXTURE IN THE INTERIOR

Texture can be defined by the very nature of materials. It can be absent with shiny glass surfaces, subtle with the weave of plain silk, seductive with a deep-pile carpet or can alert you to danger with a splintered wood surface. Surface textures can be cold or warm to the touch (compare the sensations of slate and fur) and invariably make a strong contribution to the atmosphere of a room and its purpose. An office with leather chairs, dark wood furniture and damask wallpaper in dark sober colours will be associated with an established male professional. At the other end of the scale, a boudoir with furry, silky and self-indulgent textures in accents of pink, red and purple might be associated with a fun-loving lady in her prime. Such associations also provide useful ways of marketing space: a financial institution, for example, with shiny marble surfaces and expensively tiled floors will give a cool, reassuring, secure atmosphere for its customers. A nightclub, in contrast, might err towards softer flooring and more malleable, fashionable textures, maybe in metallic or plastic materials that sparkle and encourage relaxation and sociability. Indeed, the level and quality of texture will often define the practical use of the room, with softer and warmer elements in rooms for relaxing and sleeping, more interactive and varied textures in playrooms, or simpler combinations where function is the main purpose of a room such as a study or kitchen. Certainly, a room with no, or unvarying, texture would be dull indeed and will provide no useful messages about the owner or about the purpose of the room.

Opposite: Although textures can be used to provide useful and effective counterpoints to colour highlights and patterned elements, it can also be a real delight to use them as a main element. This pale interior revels in the subtle textures of fabrics, tiles, organic forms and the matt quality of the walls.

Surface texture and the light around it plays an important role in delineating depth and spaciousness. A textured three-dimensional surface, such as coir matting, will have a characteristic structure and presence when observed close to, but seen from a distance it might merge into the surrounding surfaces, just creating an impression of a colour with no definable texture. Even coarse textures appear to be smoother when viewed from a significant distance, although these will also make a plane seem closer and therefore increase its impact. The same applies to wall-mounted textures: the effect of mounting a woven rug or tapestry on a distant wall will be quite different to seeing it close up in a small room.

In the same way as light affects how we see colour (*see pages* 64–65), it also changes the physical impact of textured surfaces. Direct light will enhance the texture of a surface, whereas a diffused-lighting system will make the texture less noticeable. Another point to remember is that the surface texture of objects will reflect light differently, so can be selected to support any imbalance in the natural lighting of a room. Smooth, shiny surfaces – whether plastic, tiles, shiny metal or wood varnished with a high gloss – particularly when in a light colour, will bounce light back into the room, maximising the distribution of light in a dark or overcast room. Denser or matt textures – whether leather, pile carpet, velvet or matt boards – particularly when in a dark colour, will absorb more light than they reflect and will therefore appear to be duller. This effect is increased by any visible three-dimensionality on a textured surface, which will

cast mini-shadows and therefore appear darker than a more regular surface of the same colour. Such textures can be used in a room to absorb and subdue harsh levels of natural light. The same applies to sound: absorbent surfaces such as seagrass or carpet will absorb sound, whereas harder surfaces such as stone, linoleum and tiles will carry sound more effectively around the room.

Another element to take into account when juxtaposing textures with other surfaces is how they are set off by their surroundings. A texture on a smooth, regular background will be much more defined than when balanced against a similarly textured surface. Equally, if the background is coarser, then the effect of the main texture will be evened out and less obvious. Of course, choosing textures for a room is also about personal preference and balance, so don't let the fact that

you love intricate textures in sombre colours stop you from incorporating them in a dark room. There are always other options for combating bad natural light quality apart from limiting the use of such textures. Painting the window surround and sill in a glossy light colour may bounce enough light back into the room to compensate for darker textural elements elsewhere, or try planning an artificial lighting scheme for daytime use to increase the light level in the room.

Generally, try to achieve juxtapositions between hard and soft, regular and irregular, glossy and matt textures. But avoid drowning a room in too many textures without having a consistent theme: one way of creating harmony is by choosing textures with elements in common, such as similar colours, similar reflectance values or similar weights.

The Café Wall illusion shows a grid of black and white squares slightly offset from their square grid. Although the squares are still of equal size and regularity, a strong optical illusion is created that indicates that the horizontal lines are sloping in different directions.

PATTERN PSYCHOLOGY

We have already referred to how we take depth cues from the patterns in our environment. Infants develop this awareness as young as two months. The fake cliff experiment designed by Eleanor Gibson and R.D. Walk placed babies on a glass sheet covering a deep surface where the depth was emphasised by the use of patterned elements down the sides and along the surface below. At two months, infants showed a drop in heart rate and older babies refused to cross, associating the depth with danger. This pattern-prompting behaviour is also illustrated by the Ames Room experiment (*see pages* 18–19), which shows how distorted pattern cues (the panelling on the walls) can deceive the eye into thinking a room is quite a different shape than in reality.

Infant development is monitored by their increasing interest in patterned elements and, as they mature, they are shown to look longer at unusual stimuli. Young babies prefer looking at normal faces in natural symmetry, but at 18 months, as they look for different stimuli to make sense of all aspects of the world, they are more attracted to pictures of mixed-up faces, with upturned mouths or features missing. This interest forms part of the process of developing an understanding of how to recognise one face from another and classify faces as 'safe' or 'dangerous'. It has also been found that babies with less exposure to sensory stimuli will not develop in the same way as those who have constant stimulation of this kind. Because young children require brain stimulation to develop their learning, it seems sensible to conclude that it is important to include patterned and other visually stimulating elements in the nursery environment.

But there is also a question of the exact level of stimulation. Too much stimulation through pattern can have an unsettling, or even a detrimental effect. It has been found that between three and five per cent of epileptics have seizures caused by environmental stimuli. Similarly, 82 per cent of migraines are caused by these same stimuli, in particular after viewing striped patterns. It seems that this is because the brain becomes overloaded by certain pattern formations, particularly with regular stripes at close proximity to each other. The Op Art movement in the 1960s, led by artists Bridget Riley and Victor Vasarely, tricked the eye by using optical illusions of movement and depth on a two-dimensional surface. Explanations for these illusions differ, but are all linked to the constant movements of the human eye inspired by the search for sharp focus, probably creating after-image effects that give the impression of movement and receding shapes. The Café Wall illusion discovered by neuro-psychologist Richard Gregory after seeing the tile formation decorating the outside walls of a café in Bristol, is another optical illusion, using black and white squares with grey dividing lines. Even though the lines appear to be slanting in different directions, the squares are placed within a regular grid of parallel lines. Stimulated by the pattern, the brain fills in the gaps in its knowledge according to what it thinks ought to be happening.

How does all this affect the interior? Well, as with most things, it's all a question of balance. Decorating all four walls of a study with the Café Wall illusion, or indeed any other busy, high-contrast, stimulating pattern, is probably inadvisable because it would distort the regularity of the room and create a feeling of nausea. Having the pattern as a smaller scale poster or picture in a room, though, or even as a single feature wall in a larger space where it can be used for dramatic impact, would be quite acceptable.

The use of tiles can be a pleasing decorative backdrop. The grid format also serves to structure the observer's understanding of the space that the tiles frame.

ROLE OF PATTERN IN THE INTERIOR

The use of pattern, meaning 'a decorative, repeated design' has changed from era to era, and has formed a large part in defining the style of each one. The Georgians in the eighteenth century were noted for their skills in using pattern in their homes with simplicity and restraint. The Victorians adored pattern and used it all over their rooms, in large part due to the ease of wallpaper availability to all but the very poorest in society since the development of the surface-roller printing machine in the 1840s. In the twentieth century, the presence of pattern in the domestic sphere shifted and gathered pace until the period between the 1960s and 1980s provided another glut of dramatic pattern exposure in the home environment, with styles definitively linked to the respective decade. The end of the twentieth century, however, saw the demise of pattern in the interior with the minimalist aesthetic that sought blank, calm spaces with no clutter or distractions. Although the start of a new century has seen a definite move back to the eclectic use of colour and pattern, most of the population still seem to have an enduring caution for the use of patterned surfaces in their homes. Despite this, the fact remains that pattern provides more than a style

choice – it has an integral role in defining and giving character to our spaces.

CONSUMER PREFERENCES

Wallpaper and fabric designs tend to have a lifespan of between six and thirteen years and sometimes even longer. The fact that there are well over 100,000 choices of wallcovering alone available to the homeowner is a sobering thought for those designing for the industry. With only ten per cent of design purchases bought impulsively, generally it seems that the consumer is making a premeditated search for patterns, tending to specify that they will know exactly what they want when they see it.

Perhaps unsurprisingly, males tend to rate most pattern designs much lower than females, preferring solids, textures and natural materials to repeating designs, whereas females prefer mini-prints, floral and botanical designs. The shape or image of the design will also affect preferences: if the motif is pointy, prickly and hairy, then it will be far less favoured. A certain type of flooring in a children's hospital in the 1970s using an optical ladybird motif actually led to repeated problems with patient balance and movement perception, problems that were reversed once the floor design was changed. Colour and pattern preferences are inescapably linked to particular periods of time, although certain styles, such as Arts and Crafts, have a perennial appeal. There is also a definite aversion to dated looks and high-contrast or unrelieved dense, dark surfaces. The current bestselling wallpaper in the UK is a close-motif fleur-de-lis design.

Environmental psychologists have found that consumers are looking to fulfil various psychological requirements in their choice of pattern in their homes, from achieving a sense of organisation and security to expressing a personal identity.

Opposite: The gratuitous use of patterned elements can become a serious design mistake. The visual strength in particular the colours, of the vertical wallpaper shown here fights hard with the vertical grid of the bedframe and the patchwork quality of the bedcover.

Above: Patterned wallpapers can be a cheerful style choice for children's rooms. In this bedroom, the heart-patterned wallpaper is co-ordinated with a same-design curtain fabric.

PERSONALITY AND OWNERSHIP

Choosing an appropriate pattern for an interior – be it a wallpaper, a carpet or fabric – is probably the most instant way of 'buying into' a given style, whether historical or contemporary. Certain styles of pattern are imbued with significance, forming part of a recognisable vocabulary. To be effective, a visual style should have the balanced contribution of all interior treatments, from the use of colour and paint to curtains, fabric and furnishings. But the fact remains that patterned elements have an individual style presence, a statement of intent that can be purchased and then worked around in the same way as a design style board. Imagine toile de Jouy and think of French country, imagine repeating wallpaper motifs of golden heraldic lions and think of Gothic, imagine a Grecian urn and think classical, imagine washed-out floral curtains and think of country-cottage style, imagine an African print and think of an ethnic-inspired room, imagine any of William Morris's fabrics or wallpapers and think of Arts and Crafts. It really is that simple. Of course, you don't have to take these 'coded' patterns so literally: you can use tartan in a cutting-edge modern context and a floral design could equally be conventional suburban or new romantic. But these styles of pattern do, at the same time, provide useful formulae to work around, no matter how the designs, and the interiors around them, are interpreted.

Pattern can also indicate status in the same way as texture (*see pages* 86–87) due to the importance of coded patterns in the past,

Any pattern design will have stylistic associations and the potential to inspire the creation of an entire visual statement in a room. Whether you prefer pale rambling roses for rustic simplicity, abstract repeats for a retro feel, tartan for a Celtic tone or tight geometry for a sober style, then use your choice of fabric and wallpaper to establish or reinforce your interior style.

particularly in connection with the church, royalty and aristocracy to establish social status. This culture of coded patterns was passed on as one of the hangovers of Britain's economic and political ascendancy and was certainly given considerable momentum as manufacturing capability expanded during the nineteenth century.

The crucial element is that pattern has an association and an atmosphere. This means not only that patterns can be chosen to link with existing formulae of style, but also that they can express personal intent and ideology. This, again, is true of all personal possessions, with the objects that we choose to surround ourselves with providing a definition of self, a public assertion to the world of who we are.

There is undoubtedly a fashionable flow to the emphasis of our pattern choices. Each consumer age group will define their own style by choosing patterns that fit with the design and cultural ideology of the day. So, for example, in the 1960s, a dramatic increase in young single people setting up their own homes in flats and bedsits created designs in response to this market, with large, bold, colourful patterns and geometric shapes. In the following decade, interior design was established as a lifestyle statement, with shiny, glittery patterns, swirls, highly textured carpets, walls, panelling and wallpaper everywhere. The approach to pattern in the twenty-first century is undoubtedly reacting against the subdued approach of the 1990s. Eclectic and often experimenting with new technology, we now have the vocabulary for a new century.

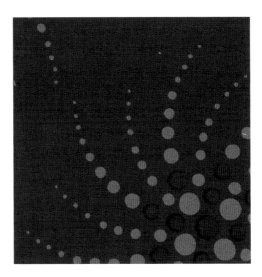

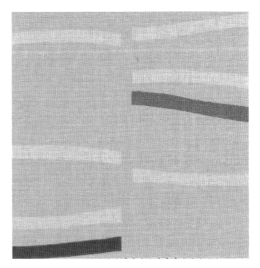

Patterns that move in a vertical direction will draw the eye upwards and can therefore extend the apparent height of a wall or a piece of furniture.

PATTERN AND ILLUSION

Just as with other interior elements, the use of pattern can accentuate the strengths of a space as well as underplay its weaknesses. It has already been established how our visual system is attuned to horizontal and vertical lines (*see Space and illusion on pages* 18–19). The vertical trigger that moves the eye upwards is an amazingly powerful one, illustrated both by the right-angle experiment and by the Muller-Lyer illusion. The right-angle experiment illustrates the power of the vertical trigger in comparison to the horizontal one. Two equal-length lines at right angles to each other, one vertically and one horizontally, indicate that the vertical one is longer. This is explained by size constancy, or the idea that a long vertical line prompts an awareness of a road receding in the distance and the perceptual interpretation that the road is much longer than it appears.

The Muller-Lyer illusion shows two vertical lines of exactly the same length, one with inverted arrows at each end and one with outward-facing arrows. The line with inverted arrows appears to be much longer than the other one. There are many scientific explanations for this illusion.

The most generally accepted follows the same principles as the right-angle experiment: the arrowheads form spacial lines that trigger our depth perception, giving the impression that one line is longer than the other. The inverted arrows line makes us think of the far corner of a square structure (as you look through a room to an end corner) and our perception 'lengthens' the line knowing that in this situation the length of the vertical shows a shorter relative proportion to in reality. The outward-facing arrows line makes us think of the near corner of a square structure where our perception once again adjusts the 'length' of the line, in this case reducing it. This shows how the use of vertical stripes, or vertical patterns of any description, will make the lines seem longer, and therefore give the impression that the ceiling is higher than it is in reality. This vertical decorative device can be used on wallpaper, tiling, applied wall decoration, curtains and upholstery with linear forms, or all of them, adjusting the perception of the height of a room, or of a single wall, accordingly to make the room more flattering. The effect of this illusion is dependent on the viewer being attuned to vertical and horizontal perspective, but this will be a well-ingrained reaction for those familiar with western architectural building structures. Choose vertical designs from traditional styles to the very latest in interior ranges.

Another way of harnessing this vertical illusion is to choose full-length curtains reaching right down to the floor rather than window-length ones. This will also create a more classical style, although other styles without this convention would not prevent its use. A cottage bedroom might stylistically need shorter-length curtains, but the vertical illusion of a longer length will not destroy the country cottage style and will certainly give more height if it is required.

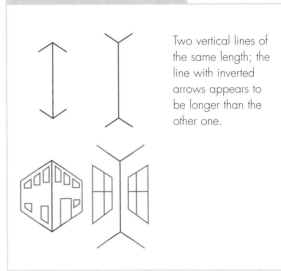

Two vertical lines of the same length; the line with inverted arrows appears to be longer than the other one.

The vertical illusion can be effective when used on rooms with a restricted-height ceiling.

There are many vertical prompts to make a room seem taller: vertical stripes, floor-length curtains, vertical beams of light, low skirting boards and dispensing with picture rails. They can be used individually or in combination for maximum effect.

Horizontal lines can also create a visual illusion by tempting the eye to move across a space, therefore extending the length of its walls or (with floorboards) of the floor area. The horizontal prompt is believed to be less powerful than the vertical one, but our eyes are trained to follow straight lines, so the illusion always works at some level.

On a floor in a narrow room, stripes or floorboards can be used to create apparent extra width across the narrow length of the room.

Although the vertical illusion is far stronger than the horizontal one, as the Muller-Lyer illusion illustrates, horizontal textures, such as floorboards or other surfaces with a directional grain, can still be used to extend the length or width of a room. This is particularly effective in a long narrow room, where, with the help of advancing colours at each long end of the room (*see Colours that advance and recede on pages* 60–63), you can lay boards across the width of the room or use textured flooring or patterned carpeting with a horizontal emphasis.

Another useful pattern device is that almost any non-geometric wallpaper will provide good camouflage for walls with surface irregularities. If painted, these distortions will be depressingly apparent, but with patterned wallpaper, they will merge unassumingly into the background. This is because texture absorbs light and distracts the eye, therefore reducing the impact of irregular surfaces. The exception is with geometric designs, whether vertical or cross-patterned, because the straightness of lines within the design can then be seen to vary from the standard regular surface. This principle applies to ugly architectural features, such as chimney breasts, unused niches, smoothing over the corners and angles to merge more seamlessly with the room. The same is true for furnishings, with non-geometric patterns smoothing over any surface irregularities or reducing the perceived size of a piece of furniture, where a plain fabric would accentuate it.

Another useful rule to remember is that heavily patterned designs have a tendency to advance in the same way as saturated or dark colours. With less dense patterns or subtler contrasts between motifs, then the effect is considerably decreased. At one extreme, the location on pages 106–110 shows the highly subtle use of colour and pattern, so that the patterned wallpaper in low-contrast colours is hardly noticeable as patterned, increasing the feeling of light and space. But in other cases, with an awkward shaped room with far from ideal proportions, the use of a dense, active pattern on one wall can really change the perceived proportions of the room for the better.

The feature wall is a device that can be used in this way. These became particularly popular in the late 1960s and early 1970s, as part of a culture that revelled in the strong use of colour and pattern. When used over all four walls, a strong pattern can be overwhelming (unless you are intent on an Austin Powers look), but the effect on a single wall can be a dramatic statement while also adjusting the proportions of the room by bringing the wall 'closer'. This can be particularly effective in rooms that are small and with no unusual features. A chimney breast papered in an advancing bright, bold wallpaper combined with plain receding walls (based on a colour within the wallpaper) will give a new dynamic to a small room and make it feel bigger. If you paint all four walls white, it may feel bigger, but you also risk making it too bland.

The final useful illusion with pattern, and indeed texture, is that it can help guide the eye to particular focal points, or rather away from areas to which you don't want to attract attention. In a small room, for example, use mosaic tiles on a coffee table in the centre of the room to create interest and distract attention from its small proportions. Or use wallpaper on the wall opposite something that you'd rather disguise, such as an off-centre door or an ugly architectural feature. Leading the eye around the room in this way will give definite points for the eye to settle on and prevent it searching restlessly around the room.

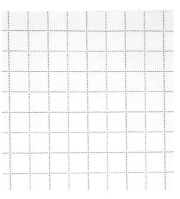

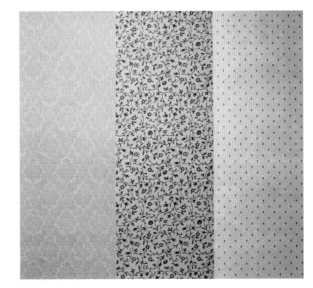

When choosing wallpaper, look at samples at a distance to get an impression of what the pattern will look like from further away. A delicate pattern with subtle colours can be lost completely, and even a pattern with strong contrasts can lose its impact.

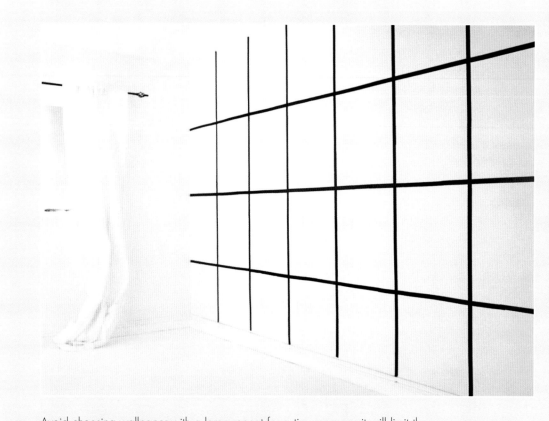

Avoid choosing wallpaper with a large repeat for a tiny room, as it will limit the space even more with the corners of the room providing an uncomfortable break in the flow of a design. The repeat marked above would provide a pleasing balance of repeats to the proportions of the room.

COMBINING DECORATIVE ELEMENTS

The use of patterned elements can never be seen in isolation. Although they will have their own individual character, their impact is seen in the context of the room as a whole, so it is essential that they complement and strengthen all other elements. For dramatic combinations of colour and pattern we only have to look to the Victorians, who delighted in the novelty of the newly introduced saturated colours in the latter part of the nineteenth century and in the new affordability of wallpaper, the definitive wallcovering of the time. We have lost the decorating confidence and the bold use of pattern characteristic of this era, with our judgement affected by recent strong trends of minimal, pale and natural, but there is a rich array of decorative and patterned options in modern tones that fall between the typical dark, patterned and cluttered Victorian interior and flat emulsioned walls.

Almost all patterned elements involve repeats. Even when wallpaper is used in imitation of another surface – textiles, marble, panelling or leather – as it has always traditionally done, there is still a subtle or strong element of repeat. The

dominance of a pattern depends on the size of the repeat, how close the repeated elements are and how strongly contrasting or low-contrast are the colours. A typical Arts and Crafts wallpaper will have dense, colourful repeats that have a strong presence, whereas with other examples the colour of the repeat and the background is so close that the motif is scarcely distinguishable. There are so many options, but each one will have something to offer individual environments and tastes.

It is certainly true that we like patterns that are designed in analogous or complementary colour palettes or with contrasting scale relationships. Think back to the idea of using colour families within a scheme (*see pages* 74–75) and apply this to texture and pattern, colour almost always being the key factor linking all elements of an interior.

When thinking about the scale of a repeat to use as a wallpaper in a room, remember that too large a repeat will risk shrinking the room. So, as a rule, use large-scale patterns on large expanses of wall and smaller patterns on smaller ones. If wallpaper has a large repeat or too strong a design for a smaller room, then it will tend to suffocate it, creating too much interest for the room to support. The Victorians, however, used large-scale patterns such as floral chintzes unashamedly, so if you are keen on a strong, powerful repeat in a small space, try their technique of using the wallcovering on the ceiling, too. Although you might think that this would enclose the space, in fact the eye concentrates on the flow of the pattern rather than on its relationship to the size of the room.

William Morris-style wallpapers have a perennial appeal. Because Morris designs now have a classic status, they can be used equally well in traditional formats as well as modern interpretations.

Patterns can be co-ordinated so that the same pattern will feature within many different elements of the room. Here, the wallpaper, curtains and china plates have a very closely co-ordinated visual style.

We have already mentioned how patterns can advance and recede in the same way as colours (*see pages* 100–101) and an awareness of these qualities should also apply to the exact combination of patterns used. You can achieve a sense of cohesion in a room and between rooms by balancing strong patterns with more subdued ones. The key is remembering your theme, whether it is a colour emphasis or interpretations of a particular motif. One of the most useful aspects of patterned surfaces is that they provide a motif or stylistic key or a colour scheme that can either inspire the colours and the nature of other elements in a room or offer a successful way of tying elements together that would otherwise have no connection.

The exact balance of active and subdued patterns and textures and plainer areas will depend not only on your taste, but also on the size of your room. If you are lucky enough to have

an airy, spacious room with a generous width, length and height, then you have a flexible template for layering the room with texture and pattern. If you use a similar level of texture and pattern in a smaller room, then you may find them overwhelming. With a small room, limit your use of individual patterns to one or two. This can be done by using bed and curtain fabric and the wallpaper in the same colourway and pattern – this provides a relaxing continuity for the eye in a small room, providing controlled stimulation that also gives an impression of more space. Avoid using small designs near large ones and equally avoid using different patterns that are of a similar scale.

The most effective balance of texture and pattern will be achieved with plainer, less stimulating surfaces to calm the visual system, and texture and pattern to create interest where it is required. Remember, though, that certain patterns and textures can be highly stimulating to some and unremarkable to others: it all depends on your individual experience and perspective. One effective idea for combining elements is to trade off your use of colour with that of patterned and textured areas. If a colour palette is carefully restricted, then there is automatically more flexibility to introduce more patterned and textural elements within a room. So, having a vibrant fabric in a plain colour upholstering a main piece of furniture and an analogous shade in the carpet or flooring treatment will give you the freedom to introduce more lively patterns, some of which will incorporate this colour, with rugs, wallpaper, pictures and other decorative accessories.

When planning the patterned elements in a room, think about where you will be displaying personal objects and pictures. For full dramatic effect, an object is better set off in front of a plain, pale wall, as it could become obscured in front of a patterned one.

Working blindly with texture and pattern in a room is never a good idea; a style board and sample sheets such as these will focus your ideas, establish the visual qualities of a room and give you an idea of how your inspiration might combine to form an overall atmosphere.

ON LOCATION

The south-east facing front room in this 1930s' house had an attractive bay window with coloured panes of glass along the top. It had a textured cream carpet with swirling foliage motifs and cream vinyl wallpaper with palm-leaf motifs in a grey tint. Because the room didn't have any seriously compromising features or significantly difficult light qualities, it was possible to treat it as a fairly self-indulgent, free template in which to introduce patterned and textural elements to stimulate and indulge all the senses.

The existing carpet was replaced with a warmer honey-coloured one and the walls were covered in a stone-on-stone patterned wallpaper in a William Morris style with a subtly patterned design. Even such an unassuming design as this can successfully disguise any irregularities in the surfaces of a wall that might be highlighted with a painted flat finish. Florid repeat wallpapers do a great job in camouflaging corners. This room suffered from various external angles such as the chimney breast and window bay, all of which were softened by the pattern. The surface of the door facing into the room was painted in cream, as the orange/ brown wood stain that was there would have interrupted the soothing regularity of the neutral colours.

This room illustrates how texture and pattern can be richly introduced without becoming exaggerated and distracting. The different elements here were carefully balanced to create a modern statement of well-behaved pattern. The two existing cut-velvet sofas were draped with white covers and dressed with an assortment of cushions in ochre, cream and aubergine (taking a colour cue from the window glass) and a variety of silky and textured fabrics. The floor used a densely matted natural rug in brown and straw colours and throughout there were accents of reflective glass and natural features such as pine cones, woven baskets, pebbles and twigs displayed in a large vase in one of the corners. The curtains were sheer and lightweight with a vertical stripe, giving some protection from the sunlight in the middle of the day. A framed picture was created to go above the fireplace, made from plaster and sand with textured gestural swirling movements.

The colours used here were principally monochrome – shades of white, cream and neutral – however, the scheme avoids blandness because of the constant visual stimulation within the sensitive balancing of the integrated patterns and textures.

DESIGN RULES

Don't underestimate the power of texture and pattern, both having an important role in drawing the elements of a room together and making it appear welcoming.

Because of the strong associations that we have with materials, textures and patterns can be used to market a space – to make it appropriate for a particular purpose or for an individual.

Light will affect texture: direct light will enhance it, whereas diffused light will detract from it. Every texture also reflects light differently, so use shiny reflective textures where more light is needed and darker, more absorbent textures where the light level is too high.

Infants are constantly searching for new visual stimuli to learn more about the world. Cater for this interest by including stimulating patterns and textures in the rooms where they sleep.

High-contrast, visually stimulating patterns can be disorientating, so use them subtly in your interior.

Choosing a pattern for an interior is the most instant way of 'buying into' a given style. An initial selection of fabric or wallpaper can even provide the colour, design and style basis for the whole room.

Choose wallpapers and fabrics with a vertical design emphasis to give an impression of more height. Use horizontal textures across the short length of a room to draw the eye across and increase the length.

Non-geometric patterned wallpaper will provide good camouflage for walls with surface irregularities.

Heavily patterned designs have a tendency to advance towards the observer, whereas less dense patterns will not be as powerful.

Use texture and pattern to create areas of interest to guide the eye to particular focal points.

Too large a repeat used as a wallcovering will make a room appear smaller, so use large-scale patterns on large areas or expanses of wall and smaller patterns on smaller ones.

Balance strong patterns with more subdued ones to avoid overpowering a room.

5

BALANCE & HARMONY

An absence of clutter does not mean the eradication of character. In fact, a clear space means that you can stimulate more attention for the furnishings and displays that you choose to feature.

You may have gathered, having read this far, that no element of an interior scheme can be seen in isolation. There is a constant fusion of elements in any room and it is unfair to prioritise any one above the other because they are all interdependent. This chapter looks at balance and harmony in the interior, issues that are relevant to all the other themes we have looked at, but also with a personality of their own. Without a measured equilibrium, spaces in our homes make no sense at all. Essentially, the character of balance and harmony is poise over chaos, comfort over unease and healing over neglect.

At the beginning of the twenty-first century, most of us continue to lead incredibly hectic lives, trying to achieve a rewarding balance between work, domestic, family and social commitments. We spend on average 75 per cent of our time indoors, far more than in the past, and our homes, as a result, have taken on the essential role of providing spiritual nourishment – offering privacy, peace, stability, protection and comfort away from the whirlwind of demands placed upon us by the outside world. We need healing domestic spaces that allow us to recharge and reconnect with our personal needs, so that we can continue to function productively in everything we do.

AVOIDING CLUTTER

Feng Shui, literally meaning 'wind and water' is an ancient philosophy from China and the Far East with advice on managing living and working environments to ensure fulfilment and harmony. One of the essential tenets of this philosophy is the achievement of an uncluttered environment. The home is seen as a reflection of the individual and if it is cluttered or chaotic, it indicates that the owner's own life may be unbalanced, and therefore stifled and lacking in energy. Feng Shui practitioners believe that if clutter in a room is cleared, significant energy channels are unblocked and you will gain positively in all areas of your life.

If you don't hold with this, then think more objectively about clutter. The nature of clutter is that it is disorganised, that it makes no sense. You can't find what you're looking for, too many things are waiting to be mended or altered and you can't move across a room without stepping over bits and pieces that have no home. More obviously, of course, a space will seem much bigger if it's tidy. The problem is that objects stimulate us, and when we have too many of them surrounding us, then they take over. Having said this, I'm not from the school that recommends sparse, colourless minimalism, which in my view is equivalent to living in a soulless box. We have become particularly sensitive to the impact of clutter in recent years because of the prevalent minimal aesthetic, but many periods of history have revelled in the imaginative collection of objects in the home. Balance, once again, is the answer. Have

personal belongings around to express your personality, but if you have too many of them, then they will not be shown at their best, and will probably be hidden and confused by everything else.

Unfortunately, once you are accustomed to living with clutter, you adapt to having it around. But being used to it does not justify it. I won't enlarge on ways of de-cluttering here, how to sort through essentials from non-essentials and find effective storage to house what you have, because there is no shortage of information on this area. What I will say is remember that you need to decide to do something about it. Don't do it all alone – the objectivity of a friend can really help sort the necessary from the redundant. Finally, remember that anything that doesn't work or is unfinished also qualifies as clutter (such as a dripping tap, a broken door handle or unpainted skirting boards) – so resolve to finish it, mend it or get rid of it.

You may feel a bathroom like this one is beyond the realms of practicality. But as long as you have a capacious storage area for all the more mundane bathroom elements, such a meditative bathroom space is feasible in most spaces.

FOCAL POINTS

I have already mentioned the importance of focal points (*see Dynamics and circulation on pages* 14–15) in relation to establishing the main circulation patterns of a room. The importance of these main features is critical. The eye is constantly searching for stimulation and focal points – often points of light such as windows, fires and the television as well as areas of colour and pattern – provide a point of interest for the eye to settle on and explore. An effective interior design uses these focal points as the main energy lines in a room. Focal points should not be positioned in corners, but be placed at the central points of a wall, on a square central axis. I like to think of the shape of a room just like a Union Jack with the cross of St George running up and down and from side to side and the cross of St Andrew running on the diagonal: St George's cross is excellent for focal points, but St Andrew's is not.

Focal points provide ways of guiding the eye away from less attractive features and towards important elements that divert attention or give the room interest and character. The majority of rooms have automatically positioned focal points with structural architectural features such as fireplaces and windows. If you are not happy with such established focal points, you always have the option to remove them and create your own. Some rooms, and especially small ones, give little flexibility in terms of furniture arrangement. In a main bedroom, there is generally only one viable position for a double bed, usually opposite the window. The bed and the window are both important focal points and balance each other effectively. If the building is an older one, there may be an original fireplace along one of the other walls, providing another point of interest. In a bathroom, your main focal point, apart from a window if there is one, is the wall at the tap end

Create your main focal points on the square axis of your room. A main focal point should never be orientated on a diagonal axis.

A mantelpiece and fireplace will almost certainly be the principle focal point in a room. If you don't have one, then you can either install one or introduce other visually compelling elements, such as a central picture or a table display.

of the bath, viewed when in the bath. So have a mirror, a dramatic picture, or a stimulating display of objects in such a prime position.

Living rooms can be trickier. By their nature, they are designed to encompass different sorts of activities: relaxation, television-watching, listening to music, children's play area, study area. With so many activities, focal points may be harder to interpret. A common mistake in a living room is to put the television in the corner, often to one side of the chimney breast. This breaks all the focal-point rules, with a dominant feature on the diagonal slant of a room. There are occasions when a television has to be off-centre simply because the shape of the room gives you no other option, but there should always be a way of avoiding it on the diagonal. Opposite the fireplace? What about opposite or in front of the window? Or even, if you have the space, creating a separate, more select seating grouping away from the main 'living' area that is exclusively for television viewing.

Focal points can be established through contrast as much as through visual stimulation. Using a soft chair in a room full of hard edges, having a bright table in the middle of the room with a flower arrangement or creating a feature wall with wallpaper or paints (*see Pattern and illusion on pages* 98–101). Focal points, however, need to keep a sense of balance. They should not dominate and distract attention from other points of interest in a room, but should give stimulation to our visual system and the space a comfortable dynamic.

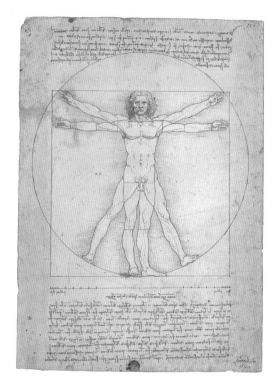

Leonardo da Vinci's Vitruvian man uses the theory of Vitruvius, an ancient Roman architect, who believed that building structures should be designed around the proportions of man. He believed that as the ultimate design form, the human body will fit into the ideal geometric forms: the circle and the square.

THE GOLDEN SECTION

This principle, also called the golden mean or the divine proportion, can be applied to science, nature and art. It was first used by the ancient Egyptians and Greeks in their architectural designs and artworks. Working on the ratio 1:1.618, it establishes how to divide a line to create the most harmonious relationship between the individual parts. This is a mathematical series in which each succeeding number is equal to the sum of the two preceding numbers. Pythagoras (560–480 BC) proved that the golden section was the basis for the proportions of the human figure, with each part of the human body in 'golden' proportion to all the other parts. The Parthenon in the centre of Athens built by the ancient Greeks was constructed on a rectangle that is five times as long as it is wide. The front elevation of the building is built to the proportions of the golden section, so it is 1.618 times as wide as it is tall.

Artists such as Leonardo da Vinci (1452–1519), Albrecht Dürer (1471–1528) and Georges Seurat (1859–1891) also used the golden section as a design principle when structuring their paintings. In the hands of such artists, this often became a complex calculation, but put simply, this means that rather than positioning objects in the centre of the picture, they should be put to one side, roughly a third of the way across.

The Fibonacci series is a connected mathematical system of whole numbers where each term is the sum of the preceding two (1, 2, 3, 5, 8, 13, 21, 34 and so on). The natural forms of nature, including the spiralling lines of a nautilus shell, are linked to the harmonic composition of shapes following this series. An awareness of such proportion and division devices can be a useful tool to create balance and harmony. In displays, for example, whether with small objects or on a larger scale with furniture and pictures, try using a rectangle where the length of the short to the long side is 1:1.618. If you measure it, you may find that your visual judgement had already established this ideal proportion.

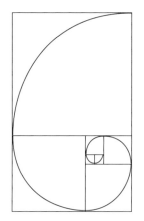

The division of square structures within the Fibonacci Spiral is based on each shape's relative size to its neighbour and the numbers 1, 2, 3, 5, 8, 13, 21, 34... This spiral is frequently found within natural forms.

Symmetrical living structures were a classical ideal, taken up again by the Georgians. Although symmetry is often undermined by practical logistics, you should aim to follow symmetrical principles in the organisation of your furnishings if you can.

SYMMETRY

There is an argument endorsed by the golden section that the individual proportions of all good design are drawn from those of the human body. Certainly, the symmetry of classical architecture was inspired by the symmetry of the human form. We undoubtedly find symmetry attractive and often use it intuitively when arranging our environment. Psychologists interpret this is as a recreation of our own physical symmetry. Because nature is rarely symmetrical, imposing symmetry on our ordered environment is a statement of control over the disarray of nature, a civilising influence on the unruly. For this reason, symmetry is associated with formality, and asymmetry with informality. It is said that we all prefer symmetrical faces, with near-perfect symmetry making a person significantly more beautiful or handsome, because it indicates a healthy diet and strong genes, and therefore good mating potential.

Above: We have a natural affinity with symmetrical displays. It is believed that this is because we are reassured by recognising the symmetry of our own bodies in our surroundings.

Opposite: Asymmetrical displays can be a challenge to achieve, but can be effective in a less formal style than symmetry. The way to make them work is to continue to balance the weight of the display from one half to the other, even though the elements are not symmetrically balanced.

Having been valued by the Greeks and Romans, symmetrical principles were revived during the eighteenth century in the Georgian era. Houses built in this period formed part of a new prosperity in Britain and strictly observed the classical rules of symmetry each side of a central entranceway. The symmetry of Georgian rooms gives them an almost ethereal perfection and the symmetrical structure allows more flexibility with other elements, because the structure feels as ideal as practicality allows, and therefore fewer visual tricks are required to make the space feel bigger or smaller or in better proportion.

Unless you live in a classical Georgian house, achieving symmetry will usually be a case of compromise. This is simply because true symmetry requires a regular, symmetrical space with no odd corners and strange shapes to upset the balance – and most houses have plenty of those. In terms of structural features, such as windows or doors, you can balance them out. I have sometimes introduced a second door to balance an off-centre door. Even if you don't want to go to this trouble, you can still balance the weight of a door or window by putting a picture or another substantial element on the other side to give the wall more equilibrium.

ASYMMETRY

Not all designers have resolutely adhered to the principles of symmetry. Le Corbusier (1887–1965) fought against the established classical ideals of architecture, looking for a new style that was not as he expressed it 'stifled by custom'. In this, he worked against the ideals of symmetrical classicism. I would suggest that asymmetry in the arrangement of furniture and furnishings is hard to achieve and I prefer always to aspire to a shadow of symmetry rather than an intentionally asymmetrical arrangement. Even when furnishing a long narrow room that disallows true symmetry, the creation of

individual areas along the length of the room still draws significant inspiration from the classical ideal.

When it comes to displaying smaller elements, either symmetry or asymmetry would be a valid choice. Symmetry is well catered for in terms of objects for display: fireplaces, for example, although sometimes off-centre are never unbalanced and are therefore perfect for paired objects. And, until the twentieth century, many objects were manufactured in pairs to cater for symmetrical arrangements. Asymmetry in smaller displays is a matter of weight: balance a large object on one side with other objects that together balance the visual weight of the objects on the other side, calculated by the height, width and density of colour of the object. Such arrangements are much harder to achieve, because the mind likes to pair objects together and create order from chaos. This is why an asymmetrical arrangement should still be balanced around the central point of the display.

VISUAL BALANCE

The houses we live in are rarely perfect: they were built for the lifestyle of a particular period with different requirements to our own, or they were built with economic restraints that mean that space, light and convenience is limited. Overcoming these problems, and we have already covered various ways of doing this, results in visual balance, overcoming the less-than-perfect to create more comfortable, harmonious spaces. So use everything that you've learned about harnessing light, using advancing and receding colours, managing space and balancing pattern and texture to achieve this. This applies to adjusting the shape of a room, but also to disguising mismatched elements within it, in particular cumbersome furniture that might have a practical or sentimental purpose, but doesn't really add to the room (*see Scale on pages* 12–13, *Rebalancing elements to extend space on pages* 22–23 *and Visual contrast on pages* 76–77).

Visual balance is closely connected with visual weight. The particular shape, size, material, colour and texture of each object, as well as the quality and quantity of light that it receives, creates a visual force. Weight is added through non-standard shapes, vivid colours, large sizes and intricate detailing. It is common sense not to put a bulky wooden dresser on the same side of a kitchen as a large table and chairs, for then you have all the activity on one side of the room, and psychologically the weight all falls on the same side. The same applies on subtler levels: use similar types of objects to create balance through symmetry, use materials to create themed connections across spaces, consider whether the dominance of individual elements is carried by the room, or whether balancing elements are required.

At a structural level, it is essential never to take installed features and elements at face value. People tend to think that elements such as picture rails, dados and skirting boards have a standard level. This is not the case at all: the height of these elements will depend on the original room and they may have been put in at a level that just does not suit the style or proportions. Rough guidelines are that a dado should be a third of the height of the room and the skirting about a quarter of the space from floor to dado. But never balk at making adjustments to these proportions to make the room more harmonious. Skirting boards may benefit from being lower, higher, in a material to match the floor, or even being dispensed with altogether to give an impression of more height. Picture rails can be fitted where there are none or their height adjusted to alter the apparent height of a ceiling. Doors may have been changed out of period, so finding ones that fit with the period and

style will give back the period context of the room and eradicate rogue elements that don't really fit in and are distracting visually. That's not to say that everything has to rigorously follow a period style, and that you can't make changes that would have been inappropriate to the period that won't improve the nature of the room. However, when the structure and decorative features of a room follow the manner in which it was conceived, then you have a harmonious space that forms a solid basis for creative interpretation.

Opposite: Effective presentation of an interior depends on achieving a balanced distribution of elements. This spacious bathroom allows the installation of the bath away from the wall to give the space to appreciate its period features.

Below: The visual balance of this room is dependent on the predominantly white colour scheme, sensitively balanced with the darker, more substantial, elements of furnishings and picture.

Above: Rhythm is created with the use of repeated elements. This technique can be used on a small scale, with reference to a self-contained display or repeating elements and colours can punctuate the overall dynamic of the room.

Opposite: This eye-level display of old kitchen implements helps to keep the observer's eye moving around the space.

Finding the right visual balance within the main elements of a room is partly about the pursuit of symmetry. It also revolves around the use of a theme that ties features and furnishings together. This might be in a patterned or coloured fabric that is repeated throughout the room, it might be in the period of the furnishings, keeping within an Edwardian or a 1950s' style, for example, or in the overall colour scheme. Following a theme in this way creates repetitive elements that are calming and logical and makes a space feel less cluttered.

Another element that helps visual balance is the effective co-ordination of materials. Too many types of materials – marble, plastic, dark and light woods, tiles, metal – will create too many surfaces with no connecting theme. So choose each one carefully, with reference to the light levels in the room and how the materials will affect it, to the colours that they will introduce and to their practical purpose.

RHYTHM

This is another method based around the repetition of elements for creating a visual energy that moves the observer's eye around a space. Repetition can be used literally with the same object repeated along a single display on a shelf or other surface, or it can be a recurring theme throughout the room, with the same colour, texture, shape or material used around the room. It can form a linear pattern, or form a circling pattern of similar elements. We need and expect rhythm and regularity, amusingly illustrated by the fact that in the Middle Ages, the burglar alarm of the day consisted of an irregular-sized step within a flight of regular stairs, so the sound of an intruder tripping over would rouse the householders.

Humans love regularity, so much so that our brains try to impose order on anything that the eye observes. If you put similar objects together, there is a tendency to pair them together, and to follow the line through to the end of the sequence, which is why they can introduce a crucial visual energy in a space.

Rhythm is also relevant when you start to think about the juxtaposition of furniture and accessories and their relative sizes. Apart from the practicalities of furniture placement (having handy surfaces or small tables near your seating areas, for example) think about their size. A large sofa should be balanced with other elements that lead the eye around the room. If you have a heavy bookcase in an alcove in your living room, think about balancing it with similar shelving storage on the other side, working around the natural symmetry of the room.

Don't worry if you have a strange miscellany of furniture from different periods. You may need to unify them somehow, maybe by stripping back painted wood, painting surfaces in similar colours, or distressing surfaces – any method of harmonising disparate elements. Alternatively, dispensing with one out-of-character piece may make all the difference. Having said this, don't be afraid of combining period elements and mixing old and new to create a more eclectic interior as this can work equally well, as long as it ties together visually.

The immaculate presentation of this bathroom is a classic, reassuring statement, with the display of bottles and bathroom supplies echoing the appearance of an established gentleman's retailer.

DISPLAY

The culture of display is linked to that of collecting. But what, really, is the point? It seems likely that the collecting urge has its roots in the primitive instincts of hunting and gathering. Collecting is about owning and acquiring objects, but it is also about interpreting those objects in terms of how they are displayed to symbolise an essence of who we are – or how we want to be seen. Freudian psychologists believe that the gathering together of objects as a collection is actually a way of combating death, of finding immortality by creating something that has a self-contained meaning. But then, not all of us have themed collections. You are just as likely to see a casual collection of objects that has been absorbed on life's journey, not necessarily with a unifying theme apart from the fact that they appeal to the owner.

We tend to think about display when all the major elements are in place: walls are painted and papered, curtains up, chairs upholstered. Yet, particularly for dramatic elements, it can be productive to plan what you are intending to display where before you decide on your final scheme. For example, if you have a large Pre-Raphaelite picture in a heavy golden frame, it would be unwise to cover the only wall where it will fit with colourful pictorial wallpaper. Or, if you have a bust in bronze or stone, decide on a background, probably plain, that will best show the colour off and increase the impact of the piece when you are planning the decorations.

Scientists have used the change-blindness experiment to prove that we don't actually pay much attention to our surroundings: we just use the information that we need. A selection of people were asked to arrange a collection of mirrors around a central picture. While their backs were turned, the central picture was switched for a different one and when they resumed their work they did not realise that the picture had changed. Taking this through to our home environments, we become so used to the familiar elements in our rooms that our minds 'edit' them from our vision when we enter the room. The logic here is that this allows us to free the brain up for new visual stimuli and to keep building up our memories and comprehension of the world. Eye movements require a minimum of effort and it is easier for us to maintain very basic information in our heads and check further details as we go, rather than storing minute, possibly irrelevant details and using them as we need them. One logical

answer to this is used in many Oriental countries, where displays are changed from season to season, adjusting the appropriateness of their content to the time of year and therefore keeping the visual system stimulated, rather than allowing it to lazily adapt to the status quo. The other way that we can harness this 'editing' facility is to use such familiar elements in rooms where we like to relax and unwind, but keep more change and stimulation within rooms that we would like to be more dramatic and interactive, such as a study or children's play area.

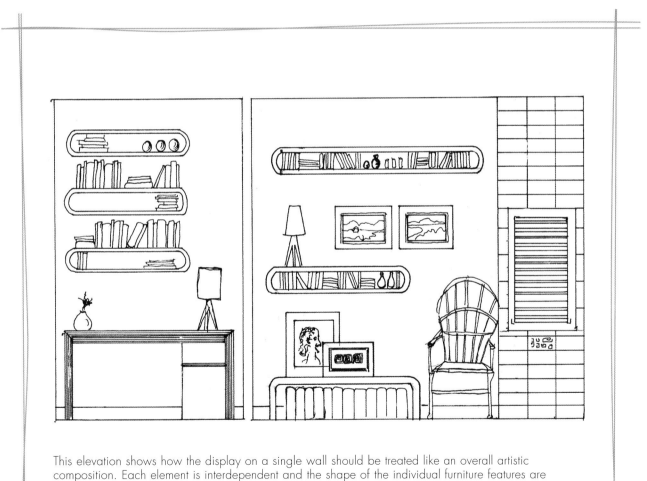

This elevation shows how the display on a single wall should be treated like an overall artistic composition. Each element is interdependent and the shape of the individual furniture features are an integral part of the whole.

A powerful display can be created through the structure of the display as well as the method of presentation. This unusual freestanding bookcase has its own distinctive character and would be a real eye-catching focus in any room.

APPROACHES TO DISPLAY

Never underestimate the power of lighting when planning displays. How much natural light will your displayed objects receive and will it show them off effectively? If there is not much natural light, consider using accent lighting to highlight your displays. Think, too, about the materials you are using – and how their qualities will interact with the other surfaces and materials in the room.

A collection of delicately coloured glass would benefit from a plain, unassuming background; a display of wooden sculptures could link effectively with other wooden elements in a room; or a collection of records might require a much more practical storage-based approach to display.

Methods of display are inextricably linked to character and individual preferences. However, there are still guidelines that can give structure to the way that you present your possessions. One useful proportional rule when it comes to a display over a fireplace is that the distance from the apex of your mantelpiece pyramid (meaning the top of the picture or wall-mounted piece above the mantelpiece) to the edge of the mantelpiece should ideally be the same height as the fire surround. This gives a really harmonious proportion to what will automatically be one of the main focal points in your room.

When hanging pictures or mirrors, you should always try to place them at eye level. Smaller sized pictures should be positioned running around at eye level and medium sized pictures should bring your eye level two-thirds of the way up the picture. With larger pictures, it really depends on the visual weight of the picture (how dense or delicate it is and how vibrant or low-contrast the colours) and the context of the room. If it shows the room off better to draw the eyes away from the ceiling (with a low-level ceiling, for example), then hang the picture lower. If you would rather emphasise the height of the room, hang the picture higher to draw the eyes upwards. The toughest challenge is to hang a single picture, especially a smaller one. It makes it easier if the wall space is smaller or if there are other pictures to form either a pair or a group display. When using a group of pictures, lay them out on the floor first and stand on a chair to judge the balance before actually attaching them to the wall. The background colour on which you are hanging pictures should not be more vivid than the brightest colour in a picture.

Think about creating three-dimensional contexts with pictures. They rarely just form a flat wall composition, but interact actively with the other elements in a space. The eye prefers to look at focused compositions, so think of structuring visual groups of furniture, objects and pictures. Beware of hanging a large painting over a small piece of furniture where the picture will overpower the composition. Similarly, too small a picture or mirror can be outweighed by a dominant furnishing feature. Effective displays can be achieved with single dramatic objects, such as sculptural busts or an abstract painting in vibrant colours. The smaller an object, then the harder it is to display on its own, unless it is closely framed by its surroundings. Using pairs of objects has great visual power, because our visual system automatically groups things in pairs and it also appeals to our sense of symmetry. This is shown by the fact that a pair of objects, such as candlesticks or china sculptures, will always be valued higher than single pieces. The other option is to use combinations of odd numbers within group displays, especially threes or fives.

The distance from the apex of a mantelpiece display to each side of the mantelpiece should be the same overall height as the fire surround; these dimensions will create a pleasing harmonious proportion.

ON LOCATION

The master bedroom in this narrow Georgian house does not have generous proportions (4 x 3½m). With a low ceiling, walls painted in a dark blue and the window frames and shutters turquoise, a busy patterned carpet and duvet, a sturdy four-poster bed and not enough storage to house the clothes and other bedroom accessories, the overall impression was small, dark, cluttered and oppressive.

The most essential priority in this location was to introduce storage that would house all the clothes and other accessories that were scattered around the room to free up the space in the rest of the room. A deep storage unit of MDF cupboards (60cm deep) with doors was therefore built along the whole length of the entranceway wall, over the doorway and along the other side, creating both hanging space, shoe storage and shelving areas.

The walls, windows and ceiling were painted in brilliant white, a cream carpet was laid and a less dominating low-level bed replaced the hefty four-poster.

A dusty pink bed canopy was made as a dramatic feature on the new low bed. It was constructed using copper pipes attached to the ceiling around which the fabric is fixed and then hangs down the vertical wall above the bed. With the bed dressed with aubergine and golden yellow covers and cushions, this creates an eye-catching, colourful focal point for those entering the room within the white and off-white surroundings. The new design of the room aims to follow the principles of symmetry and where this is not possible, then to ensure a sense of balance and control. Usually within bedrooms, particularly smaller ones, there is far less flexibility to adjust the position of the furniture than with other rooms, with there often being only one feasible position for a double bed, for example. But even with these restrictions, there is still ample opportunity to edit out clutter and guide the eye through the room towards attractive features rather than letting it dwell on less desirable elements.

The Chinese system of Feng Shui maintains that a bedhead should always be against a wall, and also that the entrance door should open so that those in bed can see who is entering. The doorway opening has been left as it was, often the way that western interiors are designed, but changing the way the door hangs would be an extra adjustment to consider in order to open up the room even further.

This Georgian terrace has a very narrow street and the windows were rather unnervingly overlooked by the houses on the opposite side. The windows were dressed with blackout roller blinds and white voile curtains (the latter not designed to be drawn). To maximise privacy as well as the available natural light, the six lower panes of the window were frosted, with the coating slightly inset from the frames of each pane. This also dispensed with the muslin curtains that had obscured the Georgian windows. The window treatment also freed up the deep window seats, previously obscured by the curtains. All painted in a fresh white, this now forms a perfect display for selected items or a private place for contemplation.

The main problematic element in this bedroom was the lack of storage space and the number of distracting incidental objects around the room that undermined an appreciation of the space itself. So sacrificing the available circulation space by building the deep wall cupboard was a small price to pay for the creation of attractive vistas, clear pathways and available surfaces for more decorative displays.

DESIGN RULES

Avoid unnecessary clutter in your living spaces – clearing clutter will make a space seem bigger, make it easier to find things and show your possessions off more effectively.

Focal points provide ways of guiding the eye away from less attractive features and towards important elements that give the room interest and character. Make sure they are positioned on a square axis, rather than a diagonal one.

When creating compositions with any furnishing elements, use a rectangle where the length of the short to the long side is 1: 1.618.

Symmetrical arrangements are associated with elegance and harmony, so always aim to follow the rules of symmetry, particularly when planning the position of the main elements in a room.

Use the visual weight of each element in your room (its size, shape, colour and pattern) to create an overall balance within the space.

Try to achieve themed connections across a space to create unity and harmony through the use of materials, colour, pattern and texture.

Alter the perceived proportions of a room by adjusting the level of skirting boards, dados and picture rails. A dado should be a third of the height of the room and the skirting about a quarter of the space from floor to dado.

Use repeating elements along surfaces or around a room to keep the energy lines moving in a space.

Plan what you are intending to display before you decide on your final scheme, so that you can create the right decorative context.

If displays don't receive enough natural light, introduce accent lighting to highlight them.

PERSONALITY 6

This period recreation of William Herschel's eighteenth-century house in Bath includes fine period detail, from the rug recreated from fragments of an eighteenth-century Aubusson carpet to the clocks and time pieces, which would have been an important part of Herschel's work as an astronomer. Such a formal style would not seem out of place in a conventional modern dining room where the owners aspired to a Georgian style.

We have been investigating a whole range of design principles that will present your spaces, with all their strengths and weaknesses, in the best possible light. When it comes to personality, the rules become much more fluid. This is a question of defining a style, an image or a mood that you would like your rooms to project. The character of a room is what makes it sing to the observer, raising it above the practical realm of room dimensions, floor plans, furniture scale and colour schemes. How you make it sing is a matter of blending function with your own personality and stylistic preferences.

INSPIRATION FROM THE PAST

Any style, however modern, will be heavily indebted to the past. This is true both in relation to the way that homes are used, which has in essence changed very little in the last 500 years, and of the visual signatures that we imprint upon them. The fashions and culture of any era automatically define the stylistic nature of its interiors and any home is part of this social conditioning. Whether highly original, blueprint designs or meticulously following the conventional fashions of the day, they are created from the same generic roots.

Historical interior styles are generally based around establishing status and conforming to conventions. This is particularly true of evolved societies whose behaviour has shifted from maintaining primitive survival patterns to asserting their cultural status. An interior style is one of the most effective ways of communicating your social background and taste, with your choice of style and furnishings identifying you with a particular social group or establishing your superiority. This is particularly pertinent in Britain where we have always been obsessed with social hierarchy. The wide use of heraldic arms and motifs in interiors is the clearest demonstration of this obsession, with the ownership of a coat of arms (which had to be endorsed by the Crown) recognised as a mark of nobility from 1484. So a Gothic style in the eighteenth century was a stylistic preference that emphasised the noble lineage of your family. A classical style, by contrast, was a way of showing your classical academic credentials. Rooms were also decorated according to their importance; in the late seventeenth and early eighteenth century it was the ceremonial rooms that were decorated most elaborately, whereas family rooms were much more basically furnished with practical, hardwearing materials.

Within the cycles of fashion and style, the same ideas recur again and again with numerous style revivals – from the Egyptian revival in the late eighteenth century to the Renaissance revival in the middle of the nineteenth century. But does this mean that nothing is original, that all ideas are recycled? No, the past offers us an invaluable heritage of ideas and as a designer constantly inspired by the great creations of the past, I would claim that any idea or even just a fragment of a style can be translated in a new context with creative originality. Interpretation is the key. Classical antiquity, for example, has heavily influenced successive styles in our history – among them Pompeiian from the mid-eighteenth century, Greek Revival in the late eighteenth century, Colonial Revival in the 1870s to the 1920s, Neo-Classicism in the latter part of the Georgian period until the middle of the nineteenth century. Yet each of these styles had their own distinct identity, rooted in the concerns of their own day and of the individuals that created them.

This living room has been decorated in an Art Deco style: the geometric style of the mirror and carpet alongside the fireplace and ornaments are all consistent with the fashions of the early twentieth century.

A dramatic bed can inspire a room's style. Here, this scheme draws from a mixture of Moorish and Scandinavian design to create its own distinctive style.

CHOOSING A STYLE

There is no necessity to 'choose' a style for each of your rooms; you may prefer just to let your possessions and your own creative intuition establish its character. Indeed, this will often be the more practical option as there will not always be the budget to buy a complete look, from the correct architectural detailing to furniture and wallpaper. If you are looking for more direction, however, then do some research on styles or designers whose work appeals to you and either adopt the look in entirety, or choose individual elements that you can imagine fitting with existing pieces that you have.

One effective way to focus your choice is to think about materials that you are fond of and would like to have in your home. If you are keen to include wood and other natural surfaces, then maybe you should be thinking of a country style, perhaps with the simplicity of a Shaker emphasis. Or, for a more modern twist that revels in natural textures and colours, possibly the organic, back-to-nature look is preferable. You might want a more formal, traditional look, in which case think about an historic style such as Georgian or Victorian. If you are keen to revel in colour, pattern, plastics and synthetics what about a retro look that emulates the style of the 1960s and 1970s? Or you may prefer a more passionate, sensuous response to colour with a mood-based style, revolving around a concept of passion, romance and theatre. If objects from foreign travels inspire you, think about an ethnic style, based on the style of countries such as India, Africa and Mexico. Maybe it is the particular designs associated with an interior style that you respond to: a liking for Arne Jacobsen's now classic Swan or Egg chairs could lead you to a Scandinavian style interior, or a personal collection of Japanese tea bowls and a preference for simplicity could make a minimal Oriental style the obvious way forward.

What is for sure is that any historical style created for a modern home, however literally, will never entirely capture the nature of the period. Many of you living in Victorian homes may live among original Victorian features, such as fireplaces, tiling and coving and you may think that your interior is true to the period. Yet, an authentic Victorian style would have been dark and cluttered, full of deep colours, fabrics, pictures and ornaments. Few of us want this today, because it doesn't fit with our modern priorities and a fashionable liking for light and simplicity. So what happens is that you are actually translating the style of your Victorian home – respecting its architectural roots, but applying your own modern styling.

There are no formulae here – it is all about choice. Design cannot all be rules and solutions; sometimes you need to respond to your personal preferences, rather than always to what seems sensible. The rules then come into play, depending on the nature of your space, but it should always be possible to reinvent any space in any genre of style.

Above: A style does not have to be closely derivative. There are so many commercial choices available to us that it is always possible to come up with something that is fresh and modern, rather than nostalgic.

Right: This recreation of a Shaker interior shows their fondness for simplicity and natural materials. The decorating ethic is one that many people still espouse today, in terms of the use of wood within interiors and the continuing enthusiasm for the classic Shaker furniture that has become synonymous with the style.

PERSONALITY TYPES

There are various theories about categorising personality types. But have you ever considered the possibility that people with certain personality characteristics might opt for similar visual styles? At its simplest, it seems logical to assume that because extroverts like stimulation and having a receptive audience, they might feel more at ease in bright, rich, crowded rooms. Introverts, however, who will shy away from too much attention and interaction might opt for a more secluded space with cooler colours and plainer styles.

The Swiss psychiatrist Jung divided personalities into four types – thinking, feeling, sensation and intuition – and two modes of behaviour, introvert and extrovert. Thinking types have very little awareness of their environment, because they are interested in ideas rather than physical realities and have a tendency to accumulate clutter. Feeling types take great pride in the visual style of their homes and are responsive to furnishings, design and colour. Sensation types are practical and interested in the operational effectiveness of their homes, rather than their aesthetic qualities. Finally, intuition types are sensitively attuned to the atmosphere of a space and often live in highly original spaces with very personal characteristics. Jung believed that each individual could be a mixture of two or three of these types, with one to two others with which they did not identify.

Another theory called Colour Affects, developed by Angela Wright, distinguishes four personality types based on colour schemes identified by the Bauhaus artist Johannes Itten. The colours associated with each type are based on the colours of nature and are those to which individuals of this type are naturally attracted. The springtime personality is lively, externally motivated and youthful and their colours are soft peach, cream or turquoise, brighter scarlets, cobalt or sky blues, warm emerald greens and pure yellows. The summer personality is cool, measured and internally motivated and their colours are cool and subtle: maroon, raspberry, oyster, rose pink, grapefruit, powder blue, lavender, viridian and sage green. The autumn personality is highly motivated and fiery and their colours are vermilion, tomato, burnt orange, olive green, moss green, golden yellow, terracotta, petrel blue, and aubergine. The winter personality is objective, focused, with strong leadership qualities and their colours are mainly black and white, as well as crimson, lemon yellow, Persian orange, jade green, cold emerald, magenta, royal purple and midnight blue.

My favourite personality division looks at two main character types: Roundheads and Cavaliers. Roundheads are introvert and are linked with the patterns of nature, science and mystery. They would like collections of things, darker colours and hidden corners. Cavaliers are extrovert and represent art, thought, light and angels. They prefer orderly interiors with clean lines that are full of natural light. All of these are, of course, highly unscientific classifications of personality and I'm not about to draw any definitive design rules from them. However, you can use these ideas about personality as spurs to make connections between your character and your taste and to help you decide on a visual route. Once you have a starting point: a particular material, a historical style, a designer's work, your grandmother's chaise longue, a colour scheme based on a painting, then you are halfway there.

Opposite: A simple approach can be the most powerful. Beware though, because any object you use in a room like this will take on increased significance and will therefore speak volumes about your sense of style.

design **RULES**

INDIVIDUALITY

If we have an overriding style in our time it is based around eclecticism and variety. Ever since the minimal style receded from centre stage in the late 1990s, a replacement with the same visual strength has been elusive. But that was minimalism's problem – it was so strong a statement that it subdued personality to an almost claustrophobic degree. The cult of personality now drives the design of our modern interiors. Freed from the conventions of an old century, we have the opportunity to follow a more personal journey – mixing and matching, choosing and rejecting as we see fit, rather than rigidly following the socially accepted style of the day. This journey should also be credited to the way the economy has grown so substantially over the past 50 years. The increased numbers of people who own their own homes, the rising property prices, the acceptance of women as an equal part of the workforce, people having more disposable income, the sheer power of the consumer – all this contributes towards the richness of choice that is available to us in the marketplace.

Even the social idea of good and bad taste has lost its edge; bad taste can be kitsch, good taste can be woefully conventional. Success or failure is all in the personal combination of elements and in how much joy it gives to its owners and those who visit them. It has been said that the culture of creating and decorating homes is part of a primitive instinct for creating and deepening bonds with friends and family. If someone adores the colour of your living room, is full of admiration for your artfully displayed collection of memorabilia, feels comfortable with the way you have presented your space, then they are part of your 'family' clan. Home decoration is certainly an incredibly strong market force. Having moved to a new home, the main priority for new owners is to cover up the old and assert their own personality. People also

undertake DIY projects much more frequently than they used to and change their decoration because they fancy a change rather than because it needs doing.

Personality, though, is so much more than a transient choice. It is a lifestyle – so much so that your rooms almost become an extension of yourself. They carry this significance because they represent so much. We evolve from our childhood towards adulthood experiencing, storing, collecting and remembering experiences and objects. Some of them may have negative associations, but others will have pleasant, sentimental, hilarious, evocative memories of the past. The historical resonance of certain types of objects, whether they are inherited or in period styles purchased more recently, can be an integral part of an interior. In the same way, accumulating objects on our travels that represent different cultures and the creative reinterpretation of natural objects such as shells and branches or decaying pieces of metal and plastic also provides decorative material for the home and demonstrates how we think about the world.

Whether you are unsure about what direction to take, or have some definite ideas that need to be formed into a realistic vision, I always recommend the use of style boards to establish your personal style and preferences. This is a personal collage board of ideas, postcards, paint chart colours, textures and cut-out elements from magazines and catalogues of furnishing elements and room styles that you like. It is a summary of what you respond positively to and elements that you would like to see in your room. It can be tremendously revealing, not just to an interior designer looking for personality clues, but to help focus your own ideas, because it will crystallise your preferred interior elements and suggest how they might work together.

Two examples of ideas style boards that help to guide the character of a room. The top one might be used for a 1940s-style boy's room, the lower one is more of a feminine statement of Oriental cocooning.

Modern materials and bold, rich colours provide a contemporary vision of comfort and protection in the same way as more traditional hideaways.

COCOONING

If there is one clue that I can give you about the nature of twenty-first century style, then it is the ever-present cult of cocooning, which started in the 1980s. In the words of the American trend expert Faith Popcorn, who named and predicted the rise of this phenomenon, it is 'the impulse to go inside when it just gets too tough and scary outside … [it] is about insulation and avoidance, peace and protection, cosiness and control – a sort of hyper-nesting'.

We've already recognised how we spend significantly more time at home and how we need a healing domestic refuge away from the incessant demands of ordinary life. It is also true that there is a definite tendency to socialise more at home, inviting friends round rather than going out for the evening. This is largely why we spend so much time investing in our homes:

they have taken on tremendous importance as nourishing, comfortable spaces where we can relax and conserve our energy. Working life can be tremendously fast-paced and demanding and having a domestic hideaway gives you privacy and physical and spiritual protection. The crucial element driving this need for privacy is that when we are with other people, we are presenting what we want them to see; it is only when we are alone that we can truly relax.

Men have traditionally been privileged to have such retreats from the world, within the home in the form of smoking rooms and libraries, but also as members of a gentleman's club. These were responses to a recognition that they needed a refuge, away from the workplace and away from their dependent women and children. Although women's needs have not been recognised in the same way, many primitive societies have periods of isolation, commonly associated with rites of passage, but also with a woman's menstrual cycle and with the changing seasons of the year.

Cocooning is not just about comfort and privacy – it can be glamorous, too. Think of a room as a magpie's nest – with chandeliers, sparkly lights, an open fire, rich colours and textures, luxury and romance. What better way of escaping from reality? Or rather, creating your own private comfort zone. This is also exemplified in the move away from complex technology and ostentatious appliances. People are now looking for simpler mechanics, unobtrusive designs and elements that help to maintain order. Elements that make your home more streamlined, more controlled, and more focused on your needs.

Whether you are considering a velvet-adorned magpie's nest, a 1950s' retro interior or an Arts & Crafts style room, when it comes to personality the only essential rule is to establish whether you will like living with it. And only you can decide that.

Cocooning is cosy, enclosing, safe and warm. It is a relaxing escape from the demands of the outside world, a dreamland in which to indulge your fantasies. Modern cocooning is really an extension of the four-poster bed, introduced in the Middle Ages to keep dust and insects off the sleepers and to offer privacy in rooms that were often shared by the whole family.

ON LOCATION

This south-west facing kitchen had recently had a new pale wood kitchen fitted. The room had quite large dimensions and very high ceilings and was painted in a brilliant white with a concrete floor, which made you feel rather uncomfortable and lost. There was an alcove in one corner, which created awkward, irregular proportions. Existing elements in the room that needed to be kept were the kitchen, the tall fridge/freezer and a piano. The practical challenges here revolved around subduing the quality of the south-west light, which during the day was reflecting off the white walls and causing glare, and finding ways of bringing down the height of the ceiling.

A picture rail was fitted around the room at the lowest possible level to straighten out the slopes and bumps of the ceiling and to provide a more intimate environment in what had been a large, chilly room. The walls were then painted a deep red, a resonant, vibrant colour that immediately made the space feel warmer and cosier. The ceiling was not exactly parallel to the floor, so the picture rail was fitted level with the floor and the areas above the picture rail left to blend in with the ceiling. Combined with the lines of the kitchen units, the crisp geometric lines of the picture rail give a feeling of control in an area that had previously felt too big and unmanageable. The areas above the picture rail were painted in a pink-tinged white to avoid the startling clash between hot red walls and brilliant white paint. Pinky-white floor tiles were laid throughout and the blind and curtain across the back door followed this colour theme.

Another effective device to bring the level of the ceiling down, or rather distract the eye at a lower level, was hanging the pendant light low over the dining table. Three other pendant lights running along the kitchen preparation area were positioned at the same height. The piano was kept in the corner niche, establishing three definite areas to the room: for food preparation, dining and music.

There's undoubtedly no better way of expressing personality than through colour, and a warm colour such as this can really bring a room to life. Why do we feel the need to conceal personal possessions that represent different aspects of our character: who we are, our history, places we have been, things that attract us, elements that mean something to us? Why do we display them in a higgledy-piggledy manner so that they can't be easily distinguished? Here we have used meaningful elements from the owner's possessions – stones from the beach, sparkly party shoes, vases and pictures – and displayed them elegantly on six shelves that were fitted in the alcove next to the dining area. If you use possessions in this way, it makes your personality three-dimensional, gives a more intimate dimension to a room and brands it as your own.

DESIGN RULES

When choosing the personality of your room, look at established visual styles. These could be based on past styles, such as Gothic or Art Deco; cultural styles, such as Scandinavian or Oriental; or your material preferences, such as wooden Shaker features.

Translate a style in entirety, or pick and mix elements as you choose with existing features.

Personality can be expressed equally well from objects that are meaningful to you as through purchased 'style' choices.

Don't worry about keeping up with the Joneses – that's all in the past now. Think rather of ways of creating your own personal haven.

Compile a style board of visual ideas to establish your personal style and creative preferences.

When choosing a style, don't forget the quality of your space and any limitations that you need to work within.

SUPPLIERS LIST

ADS Window Films
Unit 4C
Walkham Business Park
Burrington Way
Plymouth PL5 3LS
01752 252583
www.adswindowfilms.co.uk

Brunschwig & Fils
10 The Chambers
Chelsea Harbour Drive
London SW10 OXF
020 7744 1440 for stockists
www.brunschwig.com
Traditional and contemporary fabrics and
wallpaper

Bylaw
The Old Mill
Brookend Street
Ross-on-Wye
Herefordshire HR9 7EG
Tel: 01989 562356
www.bylaw.co.uk
Furniture

Christopher Wray
600 Kings Road
London SW6 2YW
020 7736 8434
www.christopher-wray.com
Lighting

The Conran Shop
81 Fulham Road
London SW3 6RD
020 7727 6016
www.conran.co.uk

Crowson Fabrics
Crowson House
Bellbrook Park
Uckfield
East Sussex TN22 1QZ
01825 761044
www.crowsonfabrics.com

Crucial Trading Ltd
79 Westbourne Park Road
London W2 5QH
020 7221 9000
Carpets

Designers Guild
267 Kings Road
London SW3 5EN
020 7351 5775
www.designersguild.com

Domus Tiles
33 Parkgate Road
London SW11 4NP
020 7223 5555
Italian ceramic and marble tiles
www.domustiles.co.uk

Electric Light Company
www.electriclightcompany.co.uk
01733 706942, order on-line
or by phone

Elizabeth Eaton
85 Bourne Street
London SW1W 8UP
020 7730 2262
Traditional lighting, beds and bedding

Farrow & Ball
Uddens Estate
Wimborne
Dorset BH21 7NL
01202 876141
www.farrow-ball.com
National Trust paint colours

Fired Earth
Twyford Mill
Oxford Road
Adderbury
Oxon OX17 3HP
01295 812088 for stockists
www.firedearth.co.uk
Paints, fabrics, tiles

Geoffrey Drayton
85 Hampstead Road
London NW1 2PL
020 7387 5840
www.geoffrey-drayton.co.uk
Beds

Graham & Green
4 Elgin Crescent
Notting Hill
London W11 2JA
020 7727 4594
www.grahamandgreen.co.uk
Accessories

Habitat UK Ltd
196 Tottenham Court Road
London W1P 9LD
0645 334433 for branches
www.habitat.net

Harlequin Fabrics and Wallcoverings
Ladybird House
Beeches Road
Loughborough
Leicestershire LE11 2HA
08708 300355
www.harlequin.uk.com

Heals
196 Tottenham Court Road
London W1P 9LD
020 7636 1666 for branches
www.heals.co.uk
Contemporary classics

Hector Finch Lighting
88 Wandsworth Bridge Road
London SW6 2TF
020 7731 8886
Antique lights

Hemisphere
173 Fulham Road
London SW3 6JW
020 7581 9800
Retro lights

The Holding Company
241-245 Kings Road
Chelsea SW3 5EL
020 7352 1600
www.theholdingcompany.co.uk
Storage solutions

Howard Chairs
30-31 Lyme Street
London NW1 OEE
020 7482 2156
Designs and restores antique and classic
furniture

ICI Dulux Decorator Centre
Unit 18 Nugent Industrial Estate
Cray Avenue
Orpington
Kent BR5 3RP
01753 550555 for stockists
www.dulux.com

Ikea
020 8208 5600 for branches

LASSCO
St. Michael's Church,
Mark St. (off Paul Street)
London EC2A 4ER
020 7749 9944
www.lassco.co.uk
Architectural antiques and salvage

John Cullen Lighting
585 Kings Road
London SW6 2EH
020 7371 5400
www.johncullenlighting.co.uk
Discreet lighting for house and garden

John Lewis
Oxford Street
London W1A 1EX
020 7629 7711
www.johnlewis.com
Home products, including furniture,
lighting and fabrics

Lloyd Davies Modern Living
14 John Dalton Street
Manchester M2 6JR
0161 832 3700

MG Sun Control Systems
1 Old Bank Chambers,
March,
Cambridgeshire PE15 8AQ
01354 651739
www.conservatory-inserts.co.uk
Window shades

Mr Light
275 Fulham Road
London SW10 9PZ
020 7352 7525
www.mrlightcbe.com

Mulberry
219 Kings Road
London SW3 5EJ
020 7352 1937
www.mulberry.com
Fabrics

Nordic Style
109 Lots Road
London SW10 0RN
0207 351 1755
www.nordicstyle.com
Swedish style furniture and accessories

Original Style Ltd
Falcon Road
Sowton Industrial Estate
Exeter
Devon EX2 7LF
Tel : 01392 474058
www.originalstyle.com
Ceramic and glass tiles, stone and paint

The Original Tile Company
23a Howe Street
Edinburgh EH3 6TF
0131 556 2013
www.originaltileco.co.uk

Osborne & Little
304-8 Kings Road
London SW3 5UH
020 7352 1456
www.osborneandlittle.com
Fabrics and wallpaper

The Paint and Paper Library
5 Elystan Street
London SW3 3NT
020 7823 7755
Wallpaper and paints from flat to metallic

Purves & Purves
220-224 Tottenham Court Road
London W1T 7QE
020 7580 8223
www.purves.co.uk
Classic and modern furniture and lighting

The Reject Tile Shop
178 Wandsworth Bridge Road
London SW6 2UQ
020 7731 6098
Discounted tiles

Sanderson
Sanderson House
Oxford Road
Denham, UB9 4DX
www.sanderson-uk.com
01895 830044
Wallpaper

SCP
135-139 Curtain Road
London EC2A 3BX
020 739 1869
www.scp.co.uk
Contemporary furniture

Shades
19 Maes Y Clawdd
Oswestry
Shropshire SY10 8NN
01691 680111
www.rollerblinds.co.uk
Window shading solutions

The Shaker Shop
72-3 Marylebone High St
London W1M 3AR
020 7935 9461

Simon Horn Furniture
117-121 Wandsworth Bridge Road
London SW6 2TP
01306 743055
www.simonhorn.com
Beds

Snap Dragon
247 Fulham Road
London SW3 6HY
020 7376 8889
Chinese antique and reproduction furniture

Steeles Carpets
Barford Road
Bloxham
Oxon OX15 4HA
01295 721000
Brussels and Wilton carpets

Stonell
521-525 Battersea Park Road
London SW11 3BN
01892 833500 (Advice Line)
www.stonell.com
Natural stone specialists

Viaduct
1-10 Summer's Street
London EC1R 5BD
020 7278 8456
Furniture

FURTHER INFORMATION

Colour Affects
908 Keyes House
Dolphin Square
London SW1V 3NB
020 8932 6492
www.colour-affects.co.uk

Feng Shui Society
377 Edgware Road
London W2 1BT
07050 289 200
www.fengshuisociety.org.uk

Techniquest
Stewart Street
Cardiff CF1 6BW
01222 475475
(Ames Room)

INDEX

BIBLIOGRAPHY

Alexander, Jane. *Spirit of the Home*, Thorsons, 1998

Ching, Francis DK. *Interior Design Illustrated*, John Wiley, 1987

Clifton-Mogg, Caroline. *The Interior Design File*, Ryland Peters and Small, 2000

Flynn, Maria. *Colour your World*, Rotovision, 2001

Garnett, Oliver. *Living in Style*, National Trust, 2002

Garnett, Oliver. *Colour: A Social History*, The National Trust 2000

Gombrich, Ernst. *The Sense of Order*, Phanes Press, 1984

Gregory, Richard L. *Eye and Brain, the Psychology of Seeing*, Oxford University Press, 1998

Kubisch, Natascha and Seger, Pia Anna. *Ornaments: Patterns for Interior Decoration*, Koneman 1998

Lazenby, Gina. *The Healthy Home*, Conran Octopus, 2000

Line, Matthew. *Homes and Gardens Book of Design*, Seven Dials, 2000

Plotnik, Rod. *Introduction to Psychology*, Wadsworth, 2001

Popcorn, Faith. *The Popcorn Report*, Harper Collins, 1991

Rodemann, Patricia A. *Patterns in Interior Environments*, John Wiley, 1999

Schoeser, Mary. *More is More*, Conran Octopus, 2001

Sorrell, Katherine. *The Art of Display*, Mitchell Beazley, 2002

Sweet, Fay. *Space*, Conran Octopus, 1999

www.guthriebowron.co.nz

PICTURE CREDITS

Special photography on pages 25–28, 49–52, 79–82, 107–110, 131–134, 149–152 by **Don Last** and pages 14,19,94,99 bottom left, 100, 101 bottom, 102, 116,129 by **St. John Pope**.

Thanks also to the following for supplying additional images: **Abode** pages 11, 16, 17, 20, 23, 32, 33, 35, 45, 46, 47, 61, 69, 71, 72 bottom, 73, 75, 76, 86, 87, 89, 93, 95, 114, 115, 119, 120, 121, 122, 123, 124, 125, 126, 128, 139, 141 top, 143, 147; **The American Museum** page 141 bottom; Hana Iijima/**Arcaid** page 64 top; Natalie Tepper/**Arcaid** page 64 bottom; **The Bridgeman Art Library** page 118 top; **John Cullen Lighting** page 42; **Dulux** pages 70, 72 top; **Electric Light Company** page 41; **Julian Flanders** pages 10, 38, 39 bottom; Fritz von der Schulenburg – **The Interior Archive** page 43; Andrew Wood – **The Interior Archive** page146; **Sue Lee** page 145 top; **John Lewis Plc** pages 39 top, 88, 97; **McDonalds Restaurants Ltd** page 40; **Debbie Moss** 105 left; **Mulberry** pages 90, 96, 98 101 top & middle; **National Trust Photographic Library**/Bill Batten page 57; **Original Style Ltd** page 91; **Sanderson** pages 103, 104; **Stonell** page 21; **Ames Room at Techniquest**, Cardiff page 18; **The William Herschel Museum**, Bath page 138.